THE BOOK

OF

MAGIC

THE BOOK

OF

MAGIC

DAVID OVASON

EBURY
PRESS

3 5 7 9 10 8 6 4 2

This edition published 2013
First published in 1994 by Ebury Press, an imprint of Ebury Publishing
A Random House Group company

The Random House Group Limited Reg. No. 954009

Addresses for companies within the Random House Group can be found
at www.randomhouse.co.uk

A CIP catalogue record for this book is available from the British Library

The Random House Group Limited supports the Forest Stewardship
Council® (FSC®), the leading international forest-certification organisation.
Our books carrying the FSC label are printed on FSC®-certified paper.
FSC is the only forest-certification scheme supported by the leading
environmental organisations, including Greenpeace. Our paper procurement
policy can be found at www.randomhouse.co.uk/environment

Printed in Great Britain by Clays Ltd, St Ives plc

ISBN 9781785039683

CONTENTS

———•◆•———

GATTI'S

HALL OF VARIETIES,
WESTMINSTER BRIDGE ROAD.

PROPRIETORS   C. & R. GATTI.

PROFESSOR

BEAUMONT

The World-Renowned Monarch of Magicians, or the Greatest

PRESTIDIGITATEUR

OF THE PRESENT CENTURY, IN HIS   ELABORATELY GRAND

ENTERTAINMENT,   THE

WORLD OF MAGIC

INCLUDING HIS
WONDERFUL SLACK ROPE AUTOMATON,
AT THIS ESTABLISHMENT ONLY,
EVERY EVENING AT 9.30.

MANAGER   MR. W. H. BARRY.

WILLIAMS and STRAHAN, Printers, 74 New Cut, Lambeth.

INTRODUCTION

T HE INDICATIONS ARE that stage magic was rooted in the great Temple Mysteries of the past. Some of the ancient documents which have survived from classical times tell us how magic was used to make statues speak and move, or to open the mighty doors of temples. The great illusionist, Hero of Alexandria, left many diagrams and full accounts of how such magic was worked. This was magic in the service of the spirit, an art dedicated to the service of the gods, rather than the art of deception.

The delicate filaments which link stage magic with the present day hint at a view of the universe which is no longer widely held. Yet, in spite of this, the performance of magic is undoubtedly a kind of imitation of the play of the gods. It is only in Judaic-Christian mythology that we discover a God whose creation was so laborious that he had to rest. In previous times, creation was the sport of the gods, a sort of offshoot of their play, and in still earlier times, creation was an aspect of love.

Stage magic is a last remnant of this idea. As he or she performs, the magician stands in imitation of the fun-loving gods. (The text in this book usually describes the magician as being a man, for the sake of simplicity, but 'she' could of course be substituted for 'he' throughout.) The magician seems to pronounce that it is all a game, a magical act. Everything we do and see is hocus pocus. It is, to use an ancient Sanskrit word, a maya. This is why magical entertainment is so thrilling – it is an imitation of the creative process, which is steeped in the idea of play.

And if magic is a thrill for the magician as he or she performs, it is also a delicate reminder of creative wonder for those in the audience. It is true that our connection with the secret mysteries of the past has been forgotten in modern times, yet, when we catch a sense of wonder in the theatre, as the magician is performing tricks, we cannot entirely forget that wonder is the greatest gift in the human soul.

❧

The Tricks

For each trick contained in this volume, I will describe the magician's performance, as seen by the audience, and then reveal how the trick is actually done. The tricks and illusions range from simple deceptions, through

'Natural Magic', to complex sleights and illusions. Some tricks at the beginning of the book are easy, and as you read through the book you will find that they become more difficult because they require sleight of hand, or sheer cunning in the presentation. Other tricks are much more complicated to perform because they require the manufacture of costly stage sets, complicated mechanisms, and so on. When you are deciding which tricks you want to tackle first, remember that whatever level of magicianship you hope to achieve, it is best to begin by practising the easier tricks. If you try to tackle the more advanced tricks before you are ready, you may well become discouraged, and lose interest in the art.

All in all, I have limited myself to describing nearly 80 tricks, when justice calls out for at least 1000. When you read through this selection, or even learn to practise them, you should remember that you are merely scraping the surface of genial deception. Now, let me explain how I made my choice.

It was the authority of the Christian convert, St Augustine, which led the medieval world to believe that conjuring could be performed only with the aid of demons. This pernicious belief endured almost into modern times, and it is this which accounts for the fact that mountebanks, conjurers and magicians (as we would now call them – though these words meant very different things in earlier days) were on the periphery of society, and often persecuted by the authorities.

Whether demons supported early conjurors or not, the number of tricks and illusions which survived the uneasy alliance between Church and Magic in the medieval period is legion. Despite their demonic reputation in the eyes of theologians, I have included one or two of the early conjuring tricks in the following collection.

My chief aim in deciding which tricks to select from the myriad was to present a good cross-section, while at the same time preserving an exciting variety. Sometimes, my respect for a particular entertainer, or a particularly brilliant performance of a trick, has influenced my choice. For example, there are at least half a dozen ways of making a bowl of fishes appear from nowhere, yet the sheer effrontery and manipulative technique of Robert-Houdin's trick has always appealed to me, which is why I have chosen his method above all the others. So great was this magician, and so popular a performer, that I have been tempted to include a dozen or so of his tricks and illusions in this book.

ROBERT HOUDIN'S WONDERFUL ORANGE TREE

It must have been a precious thing to have been alive in France in the 1850s, and have visited Robert-Houdin's 'Soirées Fantastiques'. During these, he performed his remarkable combination of tricks, advertised under the name of 'The Wonderful Orange Tree'. Some of his contemporaries wrote of their experience of mystery in seeing this performed by the master. Fortunately, in his autobiography, Robert-Houdin has left us a detailed account of how he performed this trick, and from this we may still catch a sense of its wonder.

After some initial magical play with a borrowed handkerchief, an egg, a lemon and an orange, the magician merged the fruit into one, then transformed this into a powder. From this, he made a solution with wine, and poured the results into a vase containing an orange tree, bereft of fruit.

Almost as soon as the vapour from the liquid reached the foliage, the tree was covered with flowers. When Robert-Houdin waved his wand at these, they were all instantaneously transformed into oranges, which the magician handed out to the audience as gifts.

Finally, Robert-Houdin explains, 'A single orange still remained on the tree. I ordered it to fall apart in four portions, and within it appeared the handkerchief I had borrowed. A couple of butterflies with moving wings took it each by a corner, and, flying upwards with it, spread it and open it in the air.'

I cannot reveal here the whole sequence of deceits and tricks used in this single performance, but a less sophisticated version of the magically growing fruit-tree is turning white roses into red ones, in full view of an astounded audience – something which Robert-Houdin probably never did.

THE MAGIC ROSEBUSH

The magician stands before a magnificent rosebush, which he tells the audience that he has grown by magic means. He is worried, however, because all the roses are white, and not the colour he wanted. I asked for red roses,' he complains. 'What sort of a trick is this?' He takes hold of a garden spray, and begins to water the flowers. As he does so, much to the delight of the audience, each of the roses turns red.

In those days, the distinction between magic and ordinary life was not as clearly defined as it is today – and who is to say that the ancients were wrong? After all, if a stage magician can make a live fish appear from thin air, this could be argued as a pre-vision of birth, of how things come into the world from secret places, as invisibly and unexplained as the magician's fish.

How The Trick is Done

This is one of the few impressive Victorian 'Chemical Magic' tricks which are not in some way dangerous and which are very easy. Before the performance begins, the magician sprays the roses with aniline powder. This dye is extremely soluble, and has the property of turning red when in contact with alcohol or eau-de-cologne. So when he 'waters' the flowers, he is not in fact spraying with water, as the audience is led to believe, but with eau-de-cologne.

ೞ

Magical Illusions

Not all the performances I have collected here are tricks, of course; some are illusions. Stage magicians usually divide their acts into two groups: those which involve apparatus only are 'tricks', while those which involve people are 'illusions'. This is the theory, at least, but it is not always adhered to. For instance, the Fish trick is often described as an illusion. Undoubtedly, the greatest of illusions is the Disappearing Lady. There are dozens, if not hundreds, of different ways of performing this illusion. However, the sheer genius of Houdini's version has always appealed to me, which is why I have chosen it.

Illusions do not always go according to plan, however. Before the First World War the great New Yorker, Joseph Dunninger, was performing in China. To impress his audience, he worked the extraordinary illusion in which a woman materializes in a glass tank filled with water, but his audience went frantic with disapproval. Apparently, he had broken an unwritten Chinese law against ladies appearing on stage in certain forms of undress, so Dunninger promptly vanished the lady from the tank.

ल्ॐ

Magical Legends

It is not surprising that old stories of performances are
still passed around in magical circles. Stage magic is
steeped in a sense of history and I have tried to convey
some feeling for this in the selection of tricks. The
earliest records of magical deceptions are in a 4000-year-
old Egyptian papyrus, which tells how a magician cut off
the heads of geese, ducks and oxen, and then restored
them to life.

The most influential ancient magician was also from
Egypt. He was Nectanebus – probably the historical
Egyptian king, Nekkhtenebof, who ruled in the middle of
the 4th century BC. Whether Nectanebus had the
magical abilities ascribed to him or not, his fame stretched
well into the late medieval period because he was supposed
to have become, by means of magical seduction, the real
father of Alexander the Great.

Legends tell how Nectanebus used his magical powers
to share the bed of Alexander's wife. He was so proficient in the art of astrology that he was able to guide his
mistress to the exact moment when she should give birth
to their son; his knowledge of the heavens had given him
an insight into the best horoscope to make his son really
great. Unfortunately, in determining the fate of his son,

Nectanebus also predicted his own death. From the horoscope, he was able to see that he was destined to be killed by this same child.

Astrology and magic merge in the early myths and histories, and it is not surprising that many accounts of illusions and tricks performed by this sage suspiciously resemble those presented on the modern stage. Among these tricks, Nectanebus created the illusion of a dragon, which glided into the presence of his mistress, announcing that he was her divine and kingly lover. By such trickery, Alexander and his wife remained convinced that the child who was destined to change the face of the ancient world was sired by the God Amnion. This must have been one of the most complex seduction plans in history.

ᘒᕽᗉ

Blood and Cruelty to Creatures

The story of Nectanebus, and the magical papyrus in particular, reminds us that from the very earliest times, stage magic has been steeped in political intrigue and violence. Unfortunately, in many instances, little has changed since those early days. Mutilations, blood-letting, and decapitations are still the order of the day for many modern magicians. For all their seeming horror, a few of the less bloodthirsty tricks have been included here, because of their historical importance.

As an example of decapitation, I have recorded one of the most interesting ancient 'mechanical tricks' – the extraordinary mechanism of Hero's Horse (see page 132). This device permits a horse, or any large creature, to be decapitated, without actually losing its head. The idea for the mechanism is very old, and the working machinery used in modern times is a perfect copy of that proposed by Hero of Alexandria, 2000 years ago. The idea of chopping off the head of a horse brings me to another point about my choice of tricks. Some of the more famous ones involve cruelty to animals, which offends me as much as it hurts the animals. I have tried to restrict the bloodletting tricks to humans, on the grounds that the audience will realize that it is highly unlikely that murder is being committed openly on stage!

For this reason, I have excluded some of the more brilliant tricks of the Italian master, Bosco, who seems to have had a predilection for this type of deception – genial or otherwise. Where the sheer cleverness of some of his recorded performances has warranted the inclusion of a trick, I have substituted such creatures as plastic frogs in place of live canaries, so that no suffering is involved. As far as an actual performance is concerned, it is marginally unimportant as to whether you shoot or mutilate a live canary or a plastic frog into a light bulb. However, the thought of the pain and confusion which the canary must experience has led me to prefer a plastic frog. The choice does not affect the trick at all. Incidentally, a plastic frog is no idle choice, for when it has been abstracted from the light bulb, the magician may squeeze it to produce a 'croak'. When done in the right way, this is usually sufficient to bring an audience to laughter and applause. Some modern magicians, who have their fingers on the pulse of the times, make a point of transforming a live frog or toad into plastic equivalents before performing the more bloodthirsty aspects of a trick.

Fish from Thin Air

ℚℵ๖

Illusions and Tricks Explained

I have approached each of the selected tricks and illusions in a way which I hope is both entertaining and easy to understand. Each is described from three different points of view. First, I explain it as seen by the audience. In most cases, I then add a few notes on the history, or the importance, of the trick. Finally, I reveal at least one way in which the trick may be performed. This last section – the do-it-yourself bit – is probably the most interesting for the amateur who wishes to take genial deception to the stage. However, the fact that I am prepared to reveal the secrets of the masters may raise a few eyebrows.

At this point, you might reasonably ask, 'Where do such magical secrets come from? Isn't the magical technique sacrosanct, and preserved for ever from the eyes of the profane?' The answer is partly 'Yes', and partly 'No'. The classical tricks (some of which are included in this book) are known by the whole magical fraternity, and the majority are already in the public domain.

This is the situation in modern times, but in the past such secrets appear to have been guarded well. When, in the 16th century, Reginald Scot wrote the first account in the English language of how certain tricks might be done, he did not know any of the secrets himself. By networking, he was fortunate in meeting one John Cautares, a French magician then living in London, who instructed him on a few of the best-kept secrets. This allowed him, in his own words, 'to laie open the secrets of this mysterie', though admittedly, 'to the hinderance of such poore men as live thereby'. Among those he collected was a decapitation trick, which Scot may even have seen performed at the then-famous Bartholomew Fair, since this was not closed down until 1855.

It is interesting that a woodcut used to illustrate an article on the Fair, published only a decade after it was ended, shows an acting booth dominated by a huge decapitation poster. Those actors would have been using the very same beheading illusion mentioned by Scot, 200 years earlier. Reginald Scot was the first, but not the last, author on magic to write about the subject without any practical knowledge of the secrets he wished to reveal.

In fact, much has changed since the 16th century: the majority of wizards and magicians appear to be prepared to give of their secrets in well publicized books. Unlike Reginald Scot, we may all sit at the feet of many masters, and learn the forbidden. Magic is no longer an oral tradition, passed on in secret (and often in fear and trembling of the law) from mountebank to mountebank, but is a substantial literary tradition. Books last longer than word of mouth and there is now an accumulation of magical secrets available for anyone who cares to search in any good public library.

Virtually all good tricks and illusions have their histories, which are known to the magical fraternity. For example, Robert-Houdin left the history of his Miraculous Fishery trick for everyone to read, in a book translated into English by Professor Hoffmann. Robert-Houdin appears to have learned the trick, in a simpler form, from his countryman, the conjuror Philippe. He in turn claimed to have learned the secret of the trick from Chinese magicians, who toured Europe in the middle of the 19th century, though the story may be apocryphal.

This potted history of a single trick refers to two famous names in magic. Philippe was an adroit performer of a trick which he is said to have learned from the German conjuror, Dobler, sometimes called 'The Witches Cauldron', but entitled by Philippe, 'Gipsies' Kitchen'. In this trick, the magician (or a bevy of witches) throws into a large cauldron all kinds of spell-making detritus, including dead birds. A fire is lighted under the cauldron. When the magician considers the ghastly potage to be thoroughly cooked, he removes the lid, only to find the water has disappeared. He then takes out the birds, restored to life.

Louis Hoffmann, who awarded himself a professorship in the university of life, opened the floodgates to magical secrets when he compiled *Modern Magic*, which is still used by magicians as a rich source of ideas. In this, and his subsequent works, you may learn not only about the 'The Witches Cauldron', and 'The Miraculous Fishery', but also about 'Aerial Suspension' (a form of levitation – see page 169), the 'Inexhaustible Bottle' (the title of which speaks for itself, the 'Shower of Gold' (in which the performer gathers numerous gold coins from the air around him, and then magically transfers them into a covered glass vase), and the famed 'Wonderful Orange Tree', described above. The revelations of *Modern Magic* were published in 1876, and since that time virtually every conjurer has owed something to Hoffmann. About half a dozen of the tricks in this book are variations based on this source.

༄

A Magical Inheritance

The English have inherited a magical tradition from France, Germany and Italy. John Anderson, the 'Wizard of the North' learned some of the secrets of invisibly materializing objects from the Italian, Belzoni. He was a giant of a man who, almost by accident, gained great fame as an Egyptologist. Before reaching this glorious peak, he had slummed it as showman, magician and strong-man, in which guise he once lifted weights so heavy that the stage floor of Sadler's Wells collapsed beneath him. The 'Wizard' found the admirable secrets of the Italian in a second-hand book stall, hidden in an old manuscript scrapbook, which Belzoni had kept, and which had been lost after his death.

The amazing Hungarian-born American Erich Weiss learned a great deal from Belzoni, and was so impressed by the French magician, Robert-Houdin, that he took from him his stage name – Houdini. Yet, although he was prepared to doff his cap towards tradition, Houdini was a determined individualist, who invented many of his own tricks, escapes and performances. I touch on several of this escapologist's magical tricks, most of which come to us directly from the master's notebooks. It is in this way that the tradition lives on, and is refreshed and enlivened.

Magicians owe almost everything to the past, and usually they are prepared to pay their respect to this truth. Indeed, it is my impression that there is a greater sense of, and respect for, living history in magical circles than in any other professional group. The magical fraternity seems to make a point of collecting and preserving the master tricks, and even of saving and exhibiting some of the exotic paraphernalia which went with such entertainments. There is an entire museum at Niagara dedicated to the memory of Houdini, while British museums and private collections are scattered with remnants from the glory of the music-hall magicians.

What should have been the greatest magical museum of all time, the Victorian centre of performing arts, the

'Egyptian Hall' of Piccadilly, was pulled down in 1905, ending a thespian era. One of its famous magical automata, Psycho, was Maskelyne's pride and joy, and is now in the London Museum. Although the tricks in this book do not involve automata, it is worth mentioning a couple of tricks which were performed in the Egyptian Hall, and which stemmed from the Victorian passion for these complex machines.

∞

Modern Magical Performances

The tradition of great magical entertainment has been passed to the United States, along with many of the Victorian mechanisms for producing certain illusions, although magic shows in the States are neither Victorian nor old fashioned. Some of the breathtaking illusions of Marco the Magi or Siegfried and Roy, are as up to date as any New Ager might wish, and as good as one would find in any period.

Piccadilly is now transferred to Hollywood and Las Vegas, where a permanent, totally extravagant magic show is performed almost nightly. In Hollywood, highly professional private shows, mounted by masters for their peers, are performed at the Magic Castle. The latest technologies, such as lazer-beams, computer-magic and the like, have been used to dress up the age-old tricks for modern audiences. The tricks in this book cannot equal the razzmatazz and expense of these productions, but several less complicated variations are described.

It is respect for the past which feeds the magical world. Some magicians have an almost perverse delight in taking the old tricks and translating them into new and more daring forms. The laser bombardments of David Copperfield – viewed almost with disbelief on television – are really stunning versions of the old mismatch and sawn-lady illusions of the last century.

∞

Magic Secrets Revealed

If the performances of the magical fraternity are so deeply rooted in the past, and their methods so protective of its traditions, why were certain leading magicians prepared to give away their secrets? For example, if Robert-Houdin was the unique master of his Orange Tree trick, why did he make a point of revealing its secret? Perhaps he realized that even were his secret known, few would be able to perform it with his panache and style. The real answer, of course, is that for a price most magicians were prepared to divulge their tricks. Usually, they would sell individual tricks to their peers, so that the secret might be preserved, and passed on, after their own deaths. However, some magicians went out of their way to sell magical secrets (not all of which were their own) in contracting to publish revelations in books on magic.

Perhaps those magicians who were prepared to part with their secrets sensed that, in any case, there are few real secrets in magic. The techniques behind most of the great tricks have been published, at one time or another, or are widely known among those who are interested in the magic arts. Albert Hopkins' book *Magic,* first published at the end of the last century, has been revised and improved in modern times by David Charnley, with a more revealing title, *Magic: the great illusions revealed and explained.* This is just one of many books which wittingly set out to reveal the methods, secrets and mysteries of the magical masters, and I have included one of the Charnley tricks.

Of course, such revelations do not mean that the great magicians do not have their own special secrets and methods – indeed, it is almost a trademark of an accomplished magician that he or she will have secrets which they will protect at all costs. The great Houdini, for example, would often reveal the secret way of performing tricks only to confound lesser magicians, who sought to emulate him. He was not the sort of man to countenance a rival in his field, and his notebooks are a mine of information as to how tricks, from the petty to the magnificent, might be performed. In particular, Houdini's work in exposing mediums revealed many of the tricks of the charlatans which had in turn been borrowed from the legitimate masters of magic.

Joseph Dunninger's work in this field, initially based on Houdini's findings, carried such investigations further, and revealed even more ancient secrets. The philosophy here was purely that if the tricks of spiritist charlatans were revealed, then their performances and financial returns would be reduced.

Although a large number of the inner secrets of stage magic are known, there are some which remain hidden. There must be secrets among magicians, for in essence a magician is one of those 'in the know'. Such secrets are unlikely to be published in any modern book on the art.

 ☙

The Skill of a Magician

Real magicians are distinguished from amateurs by 'what they know', and the skill with which they use this knowledge. It is true that, in a sense, we are all magicians in so far as we know the rule about the missing domino, and are prepared to turn this knowledge into a trick – but this does not qualify us to catch goldfish from empty air. However much we know, if we lack skill, then we are not true magicians – we remain what the masters call 'parlour performers' or 'false bottom' men, because the tricks rely upon apparatus, rather than upon dexterity, mental ability, or showmanship.

This does mean that there is one element in stage magic which is far more important than the 'secrets'. This is something which can never be revealed, never given away, for it is simply superior skill and dexterity. 'The secret of success as a conjuror', wrote Robert-Houdin, 'requires three things – first, dexterity; second, dexterity; and third, dexterity.'

The ability to practise sleight of hand, to makes cards move and change according to one's whim – this is the true art of the magician. Though this kind of legerdemain may partly be a gift, it is really an acquired art: it may be learned only at great expense of time and labour. If you think this is not the case, then try mastering a relatively simple technique, such as Vanishing a Coin (see page 73), and you will see how difficult real magic can be. Spend an hour or so each day for a couple of weeks, and then reflect that you are working on only one of maybe 200 deceptions upon which the magical repertoire rests. If you are happy with your progress, then try your hand at Robert-Houdin's Miraculous Fishery trick – and remain humble!

This book is written for those who recognise that they are not, and never will be, performers of the Fish trick, yet wish to know something of the secrets of stage magic, and even put on a show for intimate audiences. Perhaps your interest will be satisfied by the revelation of some of the secrets: perhaps you will be sufficiently enthused to try

Musée Grévin
MAGIE NOIRE
APPARITIONS
instantanées
PAR LE PROFESSEUR CARMELLI

some of the tricks for yourself. Whatever your initial interest, however, I hope that you will appreciate the extraordinary effort of imagination which goes into the art of magic.

The real 'magic' in stage magic is the inventive imagination of the magician. In fact, it is no accident that the word 'magic' has the same root as 'image', which, in turn, gave us the word 'imagination'. Our imagination is really our faculty of building pictures, of making images. Stage magic, on whatever level it is practised, is the art of making pictures. The truth is that the pictures which the magician makes do not correspond with reality. A really clever magician can create in your mind a picture of a woman being done to death with a saw-blade, or of a frog being shot from a gun, while, all the time, the woman is quite comfortable and untouched by the saw, and the frog is not being projected at high speed through the air. There is a conflict between imagination and reality – yet which is real, and which is false?

The genuine magician is a dealer in images. With a fertile imagination, the gifted performer can create more and more extraordinary images to astound and entertain an audience. A truly brilliant magician can so override the normal sequence of events that his images, when taken literally, can offend. All too frequently, when a lady is sawn in half (and especially when this involves a liberal flow of 'blood') members of the audience may faint. It is their own imagination which takes them into this swoon, but their imagination must collude with the magician. On a less dramatic level, there are records of magicians being pursued, even by the law, for the supposed cruelty they practised on their animal and human victims.

When does a magician take a trick or illusion too far? There are many tricks and illusions which could be developed to a point where they would offend good taste. Few more compelling examples may be given than the act performed by Lafayette, at the turn of the century, in the guise of Dr Kremser, if only because this was openly advertised as a 'Vivisectionist' act. The electrifying performance was not quite what the audience might have expected, however, for while the hypnotist-surgeon, Dr Kremser, set out to vivisect a dog, it was the doctor himself who lost his head at the paws of the canine creature. It was all good melodrama, but was it legitimate magical entertainment, one wonders?

Another Victorian stage trick, made famous by Bosco, in which the magician bit off the head of a canary, is a case in point. A contemporary who was present at such a performance spoke, with some enthused horror, of the blood which dripped from his own fingers when he handled the bird. The fact that Bosco was dealing in illusions, in unreal pictures, did not deter his critics. Assuming that the magician is dealing with pictures – and with unreal pictures – can he or she take things too far?

The Bird-Cage Trick of Carl Hertz of San Francisco was justly famous in his day. In essence, the trick consisted of Hertz holding a small cage in which was a live canary. Both cage and bird would disappear, even as he held it. Some people believed that he killed the bird in order to perform the trick, and eventually, in 1921, Hertz was summoned to present evidence before a Select Committee to give an account of what he did with his canaries. The magician duly performed the trick with a canary which had been especially marked, and convinced his audience that he was not being cruel to birds.

The modern Swiss magician, Ravisoud, has performed the most gruesome acts with a circular saw, cutting through the flesh of a scantily dressed assistant. While some members of the audience could not bear to look at what was happening on stage, at the end of the act, the woman was always there, in one piece, to take her bow alongside the great performer. In the end, magic is a question of 'seeing is believing'. Who can draw a line where imagination ends and reality begins?

CHAPTER 1

SIMPLE TRICKS FOR BEGINNERS

Very few magic tricks can be described as 'easy' but some are undoubtedly less difficult than others. The key to success is to practise, practise again and keep practising. You should never try to perform a trick unless you feel completely confident. Another professional tip is that it is best not to challenge your audience to guess how a trick is done. Both you and the audience know that deception of some sort is involved, but if you talk confidently and humorously while you are entertaining everyone, the performance is more likely to be a magical success.

The Magic Bottle

The magician hands a member of the audience an opaque bottle, preferably covered in magical symbols. This, he explains, is a sacred spirit bottle from China, used in magical rituals. The participant ensures that the bottle is empty.

The magician drops into the neck of the bottle a short rope, pulling it up and down to show that it is an easy fit. Then he turns the bottle over, and wiggles the rope again. When he turns the bottle back to its upright position, the rope pulls tight – and, much to everyone's astonishment, the rope stays in place. The magician grasps the end of the rope firmly to pull it upwards. The bottle is raised from the floor or table and is suspended in mid-air.

HOW THE TRICK IS DONE

While showing the bottle to the audience, the magician palms an ordinary ball of wool, small enough to drop into the neck of the bottle. When he pushes the end of the rope into the bottle, he also drops in the ball of wool.

While the rope and woollen ball will slip into the bottle neck individually, they will not fit in together. When the bottle is turned upside down, the ball rolls down towards the neck, and meets up with the rope. Thus, both begin to contend with each other to fall out, but are held in place, the one by the other.

If the magician tugs on the rope, both rope and wool will jam firmly into the neck. This is what enables the magician to swing the rope with the bottle attached to it. When, at the end of the trick, he wishes to free the rope, he places the bottle on the floor or table, pushes the rope down slightly (thereby releasing the ball of wool), and pulls out the rope.

കൗ

A Magic Wand Trick

The magician casually holds out his hand towards the audience, to show that it is empty. With his other hand, he throws the magic wand into the air, to prove that it is not attached to anything. Supporting his left hand with his right, as though to steady it, he balances the wand upon the outstretched palm of his left hand. He then begins to twist his hand. The audience anticipates that the wand will slip off, but even when the palm of the hand is vertical, the wand remains magically in place.

HOW THE TRICK IS DONE

As he turns the palm of his left hand away from the audience, the magician lays the forefinger of his right hand across it, and over the wand. In this way, the wand will stay in place no matter what angle it is at.

❧

A More Advanced Magic Wand Trick

The magician who has just completed the previous trick may do a double-take, a sort of genial con. He may, as though by accident, reveal the previous trick to his audience, by allowing everyone to see the forefinger of his right hand holding the wand in place. At this 'discovery', the magician may pretend to be embarrassed. He might even apologize. A better wheeze, however, is for him to severely admonish his middle finger for fooling everyone.

Once again, he tries the trick, appearing to repeat it in exactly the same manner. However, this time, just as the palm of his left hand is beginning to move into a dangerous incline, he draws back his right hand completely. He continues to rotate his palm, still carrying the wand. Now the audience expects the magic wand to slide off his palm. Much to their surprise, however, it does no such thing.

When the wand is vertical, and still carried by the palm, the magician slowly swings round his left hand to show that the wand is, indeed, magically levitating, unsupported by anything.

HOW THE TRICK IS DONE

There are several ways of doing this trick, but this is one of the most frequently used methods.

The magic wand has a retractable nail, set into it, about half-way down its length. While he is apologizing to the audience for his previous mistake, or while he is blaming his middle finger, the magician slips out this nail, and drops it into the space between the middle finger and ring finger of his left hand. The audience will be so intent on expecting a repetition of the previous trick that they will not be inclined to observe any such trickery.

✿

Finding a Card

The magician deals out nine playing cards into three rows, and asks a member of the audience to choose a card. The magician takes this card and places it with the other cards, for shuffling. He turns his back, and asks the participant to deal out the cards once more, as before. Once this is done, the magician turns round, and immediately identifies the card previously chosen.

He asks another member of the audience to change the position of the card with any other in the set of nine. Again, this is done while the magician turns his back, and when he turns round, he immediately identifies the chosen card.

HOW THE TRICK IS DONE

Here is a simple way to perform the trick, although there are many variations.

When the magician takes the chosen card to look at it, he presses his index finger on the back. In this way, he transfers a tiny black spot on to the card, ensuring that he can identify it later, with ease.

ॐ

Feeling a Card

THE MAGICIAN ANNOUNCES that he is so sensitive that he is able to identify cards simply from their feel. To prove this, he spreads a number of cards (perhaps half a deck) on a baize table. One of the cards is selected by a member of the audience, who shows it to everyone except the magician. The card is handed back to the magician so that he cannot see its face-value.

To familiarize himself with the card, the magician strokes its back. He then places it in the pack, which he gives to a member of the audience to shuffle.

When the cards are returned to him (well shuffled), the magician runs his finger over one or two of the cards until he locates the one which had been identified earlier.

HOW THE TRICK IS DONE

When the chosen card is handed back to the magician, before the shuffling, he makes a small dent in its edge with his fingernail. It is this nicked card which he seeks when running his fingers over the backs of the pack, pretending to feel for the right card.

❦

The Disappearing King

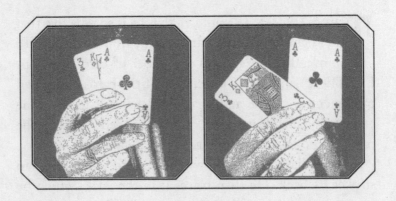

The magician holds up three fanned cards. At the centre is a King of Diamonds. He turns the cards over, and asks a member of the audience to remove the King, and put it in his or her pocket, without looking at it, or the magic will not work.

This completed, the magician then asks the participant to take the King out of the pocket. However, much to the mystification of all, the card which emerges is not the King but one of the other two cards. The magician goes back to his own pack, to show that there are still three fanned cards, with the King at the centre.

HOW THE TRICK IS DONE

This amusing deceit needs a small amount of preparation, but remains one of the simplest of card tricks.

There is no real King in the fanned set at all. Prior to the trick, a King of Diamonds has been cut diagonally in half, and glued over one of the other cards. When fanned, with another card in front of it to hide the cut, the illusion is of three complete cards.

To complete the trick, the magician includes a fourth card. This is a spot card, which is identical to the front card and aligned behind it so perfectly that it is not visible.

When the 'three' fanned cards are turned over, the magician moves the aligned card, so that three backs are visible. The participant is asked to remove the King, and quite naturally picks out the middle card.

ⓧ

The Torn Sheet

The magician holds up an envelope and takes from it a folded sheet of paper. In full view of the audience, he tears it into many pieces, and rolls these into a ball. Almost immediately, he unrolls the ball. Much to the surprise of the audience, the sheet of paper is found to be intact. He screws this up, and pops it into his pocket.

This trick may be performed with many different types of paper. For example, the idea of tearing up a school report usually goes down well with audiences of children. On the other hand, bills are popular with adults. In either case, when the report or bill is restored intact, there is usually a groan from the audience, mingled with a sense of wonder.

HOW THE TRICK IS DONE

There are three identical sheets of paper. One is folded in advance, to a small size. With the folds outwards, this small wad is glued lightly to the back of another sheet.

When the intact sheet is first shown to the audience, the magician covers the folded sheet with his thumb. The tearing of the first sheet is done slowly and systematically, with each torn sheet being placed in front of the sheet which has the folded wad on its back. Eventually, as the tearing proceeds, the torn sheets become the same size as the folded sheet. At this point, deftly covering his action with patter, the magician turns the folded sheet to the front.

Holding the torn sheets firmly against the back of the wad, the magician unfolds this to reveal the sheet 'restored' to its original form. He then crumples this up, and puts it into a pocket.

One essential part of the preparation is that the magician should have a third, identical, sheet already crumpled in his pocket. This may be required if someone wants to examine the paper, after the trick is done. Of course, it would be bad theatre to offer this third sheet from your pocket without a specific request. If you are asked to show it, do so most reluctantly, as though you feel somewhat offended that your magical ability should be challenged in this manner.

❧

Kellar's Straw Trick

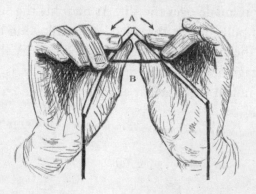

This is one of a few tricks which preserves the name of its inventor – in this case, the American magician, Kellar (1849-1928). It is more usual for names to be abandoned in time.

The magician takes an ordinary drinking straw, and threads through it a length of coloured string. This is done in full view of the audience. He bends the straw in half, and cuts through the folded 'V, about 2.5 cm (1 in) down, or directly on the fold itself.

When he opens out the bent straw, the string is miraculously uncut.

HOW THE TRICK IS DONE

Before the performance, the magician cuts the middle 10 cm (4 in) of the drinking straw with a razor. When he holds the threaded straw up, prior to folding it into a 'V, he ensures that this cut is facing downwards. The 'V'-fold is therefore made over the slit. As he folds the straw, the magician pulls on the threaded string, allowing it to slip through the cut, to form the cross-bar of an 'A' shape. By this stratagem, when the top apex of the 'V is cut, the string is not in the straw at all, and therefore remains in one piece.

൚

Cutting a 'Lady' in Two

The magician takes a pack of ordinary buff envelopes, with the flaps across their shorter side. He hands these to members of the audience, who examine them at their leisure. When these have been returned to the magician, he slips from this pile a single envelope.

Depending on how he wishes to dramatize the act, he selects a picture of a woman, which he may have cut out from a magazine, or which perhaps he has drawn in advance. It can be more fun if the audience is allowed to select which image is to be cut in half, in which case the magician can display a selection of pictures for them to choose from, and encourages everyone to make the choice with a stream of relevant patter. Of course, the 'victim' does not have to be an anonymous woman, although the traditional magic trick involves sawing a woman in half. For instance, the magician might propose famous political personalities for mutilation.

When the choice has been made, the magician slips the woman or whoever, into the envelope. He seals the envelope, if he wishes, or he leaves the feet of the woman sticking out, to prove that she is still inside. Now, the magician takes a pair of scissors, and cuts the envelope across the middle. He holds up the two halves for the audience to see. Then, without more ado, he puts the two halves together again, and pulls out from the envelope the uncut woman. Although the envelope is definitely in two pieces, the image has somehow managed to survive unscathed!

HOW THE TRICK IS DONE

This trick is simplicity itself. The envelope which the magician selects from the pile, and which he has secretly marked so that he can identify it, has been tampered with. Before the show, the magician makes a slit across the back of the envelope, in about the same place where he plans to cut during the trick.

When he inserts the image of the intended victim, he carefully makes sure that half the image slides through this slit and remains on the outside of the envelope. The audience believes that it is on the inside, and the magician must hold up the envelope to encourage this belief.

Before he puts the scissors to paper, the magician bends over the image and holds it so that it cannot be seen by the audience. Thus, when he cuts across the envelope, he misses the image altogether. When displaying the two halves, he must be sure to keep the front of each directed towards the audience. Once he has placed the two halves back together again, he merely opens the flap and pulls the image out of the envelope in one piece.

It is quite possible to include a little 'blood' letting in this act. Towards this gory end, a small sac of red ink, covered in a skin-coloured plastic, needs to be palmed, or stuck to the magician's left hand. At the beginning of the scissor cut, he nicks this plastic with the point of the scissors, and then shows great surprise when 'blood' starts to drip from the envelope.

Balancing a Wine Glass

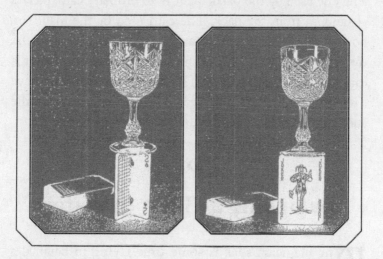

The magician invites a member of the audience on stage and hands him or her a wine glass, along with a pack of playing cards. The person's task is to hold the card upright, balance the glass on it, and then take away the hand which is supporting the card. This cannot be done without the glass and card falling over, much to the annoyance of the participant and amusement of those watching.

Taking the same playing card, the magician tries his own skills. After a few failures, he finally succeeds in balancing the glass on the upright card, and is able to take his hand away.

HOW THE TRICK IS DONE

The key to success lies in the playing card, which the magician switches without arousing the audience's suspicions. The one used by the participant is an ordinary card, picked at random from the pack. The card used by the magician, however, has a hidden flap at the back, which allows the card to stand upright. Once the card is a simple tripod, it is easy to stand the glass on it. The magician pretends to have a few failures at the beginning, because he does not want the audience to see that, for him, the trick is a piece of cake.

❧

Balancing a Glass of water

The magician spends some time trying to balance a glass of water at a precarious and impossible angle on a cloth-covered table. Much to the astonishment of the audience, he finally succeeds. He leaves the glass in this position for a moment or two, and then hands it to a member of the audience, inviting them to try the same trick. No one is able to make the glass balance.

HOW THE TRICK IS DONE

Houdini used to perform this trick, which is designed for an intimate audience and is perhaps best done at the dinner table.

Before performing the trick – and unknown to those present – the magician places an ordinary matchstick under the tablecloth, in the position where he plans to balance the glass. He has also tied to the matchstick a fine thread, which is long enough to hang over the edge of the table and down under the tablecloth. With the matchstick as a hidden support, it is easy for the magician to place the glass so that it is leaning at a precarious angle. The magician removes the matchstick before anyone else tries to balance the glass, by pulling on the thread. When he hands the glass to a member of the audience, everyone's attention is directed away from the table, so no one will see him pulling the thread and the match with it.

❧

Balancing an Egg

The magician explains to the audience that he has perfected the art of balance and can do many impossible tricks. He holds out a basket of eggs, and invites someone in the audience to select one. He then takes a stick and asks him or her to balance the egg on its rim.

Not surprisingly, the participant fails to perform this task. Once he or she has admitted defeat, the magician takes another egg from the basket and, after a few attempts, succeeds in balancing it on the rim of the stick.

HOW THE TRICK IS DONE

The egg chosen by the person in the audience is a normal fresh egg. If he or she cracks or breaks any eggs while trying to do the trick, this only confirms to others watching that they are real. The egg used by the magician, however, is not what it seems.

Before performing the trick, the magician blows an egg. To do this, you need to make a small hole – with a large needle or drawing pin – in both ends and then blow gently through one end to expel the contents through the other hole. If you do this carefully, the hole through which the raw egg passes should not get much larger. Once the egg is 'blown', fill it with water, and swill it around to clean the inside. Leave it to dry thoroughly, then seal the hole at the thicker end with candle-wax.

Now, using a small funnel of paper, pour fine sand through the hole at the thinner end of the egg, until the shell is about an eighth full. Seal the remaining hole with wax. Use fine sandpaper to smooth the surface and then paint it with matt acrylic to match the colour of the shell.

Because this operation changes the egg's centre of gravity you will find that it will stay upright in all sorts of unlikely places – from the edge of a table, to a knife or a wine glass. If you are trying to balance it on something narrow, like the rim of a glass, you will need to shake the egg (imperceptibly to the audience, of course) to settle the sand inside on a horizontal plane. This will ensure that the egg remains balanced on a vertical axis.

In an amusing – but slightly more difficult – alternative to this trick, the magician balances the egg on the tip of his wand, held vertically. Since the wand is only as steady as the hand which is supporting it, some degree of genuine balance is required. It helps if the end of the wand is slightly concave, so that the egg can sit on it, and takes only a little practice to master the trick.

❧

Two Balancing Eggs

The magician asks a member of the audience to choose two eggs from a basket. He or she must then try to balance one egg on top of the other, either on a table or even with the bottom egg safely held in an egg cup. However much the participant tries, he or she will not succeed.

The magician takes one of the eggs from the participant and, with great care, balances this in the middle of the table. He then takes another egg from the basket, and balances this on top of the first egg. Finally, he takes a third egg, or some other small object, and balances this on top of the other two.

HOW THE TRICK IS DONE

The egg which is balanced on top of the first has been blown and filled with sand, as described in the previous trick. The low centre of gravity makes it simple to balance it on the bottom egg. If you want to balance a small object on top – a chess piece, for example – you simply need to stick a piece of double-sided tape on its base in advance.

A professional magician might use a pivoted lever, hidden beneath the table, to perform a variation of this trick. When the lever is pressed (unseen, of course, by the audience), a fine needle is pushed through the top of the table. The magician then takes the egg from the participant and presses it onto the needle, under the pretext of trying to balance it. The needle holds the egg firmly in place.

The lever is not really necessary however. It is just as easy to arrange, in advance, for a short needle to be sticking through the tablecloth, with the eye end embedded into the wood of the table underneath. The audience will not see the obtruding point, especially if you get them to try to balance the eggs on another part of the table. The egg which you try to balance first must be hard-boiled. When this is placed over the point of the needle, it will be held upright. If you think that it is going to be difficult to select the hard-boiled egg without detection, there is no harm in all the eggs being hard-boiled.

෪

The Moving Ball

The magician hands around a small ball, a few inches in diameter, so that the audience may examine it and ensure that there is nothing unduly magical about it. When he has got the ball back, he places it on the table and waves over it his magic wand, or his 'magnetized' fingers.

Slowly, the ball begins to roll across the top of the table, following the direction of his wand or fingers. Before the ball reaches the edge of the table, the magician takes a handkerchief and places it in the path of the ball. When the ball reaches the handkerchief, he takes it by the four corners and lifts the ball. Then he hands the ball and handkerchief to the audience, for further examination. No one can see how the magic worked.

HOW THE TRICK IS DONE

The great Houdini favoured this trick and called it the 'Spooky Ball'. Like many simple tricks, it is best performed in front of an intimate audience. When he is preparing his act, out of sight of the audience, the magician hides under the tablecloth a thin ring, to which a thread is attached. The thread stretches to the far side of the table, where its end is ultimately held by an accomplice. At the beginning of the trick, the magician places the ball directly over the ring. When the accomplice pulls the thread, the ring is dragged across the table, taking the ball along with it.

When the magician picks up the ball, it is not really to prevent it from rolling off the edge but to obscure the fact that it is on the ring. As the magician lifts the handkerchief and ball, the accomplice pulls out the ring and hides it.

෴

Restoring a Burned Card

The magician asks for a volunteer to step forward. He gives this participant a sealed envelope, and asks him or her to place it in a pocket, where no one may have access to it. Now the magician asks the participant to select a playing card at random from a pack and show it to the audience.

The magician takes the card, holds it up so that it is in full view, and tears it into small pieces. He selects a single torn corner, and puts it in a second envelope which he also asks the participant to keep safe. Alternatively, he may do without the envelope and simply hand the piece over.

To complete the trick, the magician burns the pieces of card to a charred heap in a bowl. After some hocus-pocus with his magic wand, he asks the participant to open the envelopes. From the first, he takes the playing card, which

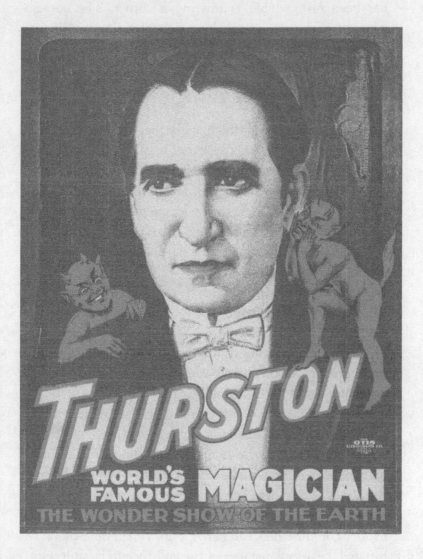

has been restored but is missing a corner. The corner which is in the second envelope, or which the participant is holding, turns out to be a perfect match.

HOW THE TRICK IS DONE

The magician knows which card the person from the audience is going to choose, because all the cards in the pack are identical. Alternatively, the magician can use a Svengali Deck (see page 231), and force the card to be selected. Before the trick, the magician tears the corner off an identical card, and places this in an envelope. It is this envelope which he hands to the participant. He keeps the torn corner for use in the trick.

While he is tearing up the chosen card, the magician palms the torn corner, and places this in the second envelope, or hands it to the participant. There is no deceipt involved in the burning of the torn pieces of card, but the mutilated card and its torn corner are already safely in the envelopes before the burning begins.

As a variation of this trick, some magicians prefer for the card to be found in a balloon. In this instance, before the actual performance, the magician loosely rolls the card, with its corner torn off, and inserts it into a balloon. When the pieces of card have been burned, the magician picks up the balloon (seemingly at random from a pile of other balloons on the table), and blows it up. When the balloon is inflated, he asks a member of the audience to burst it with a pin, at which point the 'restored' card will fall dramatically to the ground.

∽

Fishing for a Card

The magician offers a deck of cards to a member of the audience and asks him or her to choose one at random. This card is shown to the rest of the audience, but not to the magician. The card is returned to the pack, which is then shuffled and placed in a box or hat.

The magician takes from the table a short length of rope which, he explains, has magical properties. He carries on, telling everyone that fishermen pay high prices for this special type of rope because it is capable of catching fish, even without a hook. Instead of hooking fish, it ties itself around them. What is more, this magical rope works not only with fish, but with other objects, including playing cards.

As he speaks, the magician dangles the rope into the box or hat, and draws it out again. By magic, the end is now tied around the chosen card.

HOW THE TRICK IS DONE

As in the previous trick, the magician knows all along which card the magical rope is to ensnare because the card is forced. The rope's magical properties come from a length of magnet, which is inserted into one end. When this is lowered into the box or hat, it is attracted to another piece of rope (already hidden in the box), which also has a magnet inserted into one end.

Needless to say, before the trick, the hidden length of rope is tied around a card which is identical to the forced one. This is why the magician has no difficulty in fishing it out when he lifts the rope.

❧

The Exploding Die

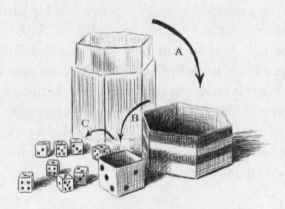

The magician holds up a small glass container, at the bottom of which is an ordinary white die. He shakes the container, whereupon the die explodes into a number of smaller dice. There is no sign of the original die when the shaking stops, leaving the audience under the delusion that the large die has exploded into the smaller dice. The magician removes the lid of the container and pours the contents on to the table so that the audience may examine them.

This trick was originally developed in Japan by Hiroshi Sawa, under the name 'Dice Bomb'. This is only one version of the trick, but it can be performed in a variety of ways which are bound to astonish an audience. For instance, Hiroshi Sawa supplied different coloured dice with the Dice Bomb set, so that the magician could change the colour of dice at the audience's request.

HOW THE TRICK IS DONE

The original large die is hollow, like a box, with one side open, and is made of thin iron. Eight smaller dice are packed neatly into this. The lid of the container is deep enough to hide the large die and also has a magnet at its top. When the container is shaken, the iron die knocks against the lid and is held by the magnet. The eight small dice, which are plastic, drop from the open end and fall to the bottom of the container. When the magician hands the eight dice to the audience for examination, he takes care not to reveal the die held by the lid.

If you have a dice set and have difficulty getting it into the container without the smaller dice falling out, the best way to do it is as follows. Load the hollow die with the eight smaller ones, and hold the container at a slight angle to the horizontal, with the open end facing downwards. Then slide the large die up the inside of the container, with the open end pointing towards the bottom. This is the only safe way to ensure that the small dice do not fall out while you are preparing the trick.

CHAPTER 2

◆──◆──◆

PARAPHERNALIA AND BASIC DECEITS

W hile many magic tricks can be performed without any special props, most professional magicians have a host of useful aids, and sometimes literally hide things 'up their sleeves'. Top hats can have pockets and false bottoms; wands are rarely just magic sticks, and clothes frequently have additional pockets for storing objects. Similarly, a table on which magic is performed is likely to have extra shelves and even a trap door in its top. Special equipment can be bought from magic shops or made at home.

Using a Hat, Wand, Table and Pockets

While the clothes worn by conjurers may appear to be ordinary, they are often especially adapted to aid the deception of the act. Until the evening dress suit was more or less universally adopted as the stage magician's uniform, entertainers would wear voluminous and flamboyant Indian-style clothing: this offered a wealth of opportunity for 'holders', such as secret pockets, folds, and oubliettes (disposal chutes). The evening dress, while not so open to obvious corruption, has been cleverly adapted by magicians to serve similar ends.

Expert conjurers usually have their clothing adapted to provide easy access to small objects, such as coins. While there is a whole battery of subtle sartorial adaptations which serve this purpose, the most popular are hidden pockets.

A standard conjurer's evening dress will have a pair of pockets at the front of the trousers, with another pair at the back. At the front of the outfit are two deep pockets. Robert-Houdin, who wrote at length about such devices, called them 'profondes', and his name expresses their purpose. They are deep pockets into which small items can be dropped and lost for the duration of a performance. At the back, near the top of the leg, are two small pockets, conveniently at finger level. This position permits the magician to abstract small items, without drawing the attention of the audience to his movements. Needless to say, these two sets of pockets are ideal for most coin tricks, as the flat and circular shape of a coin permits it to slide in and out, unobtrusively and easily, between the fabric folds.

Undoubtedly, the most famous articles of clothing in magical entertainment are the conjurer's own cuffs. 'You have it up your sleeve!' is a frequent refrain when sharp-eyed children are being entertained by an amateur magician. This potential challenge is one good reason why the experienced magician tries to avoid hiding coins up his sleeve, except when it is absolutely necessary.

There are one or two rather crude devices used by lesser magicians to ensure that a coin may be vanished up the sleeve, or into other parts of clothing. These usually involve coins into which small holes have been bored, to take one end of a fine length of elastic. The other end of the elastic is firmly tied to the top part of the inner sleeve, so that when the coin is held in the hand, it is under some tension from the elastic. When released by the fingers, the coin will fly back into the sleeve with such speed that its movement will not be detected by the audience.

A most interesting alternative to the elastic string is much more refined in its application. In this vanishing trick, the holed coin is attached to a length of ordinary black cotton, or special invisible thread which may be purchased at magic shops. The string is passed up the right sleeve, through the inside back of the coat, with the other end fixed about half-way down the right sleeve (at about elbow level). The conjurer holds up the coin in the fingers of his right hand. When he moves up his left arm, as though to wave a magic pass, the string pulls the coin from the grasp of his fingers, and down into the sleeve, where it will remain hidden for the duration of the performance.

The collar is a clever alternative to the sleeve as an oubliette for coins. The magician stands in such a position that he is presented three-quarters on to the view of the audience, who have a sight of his left side. As we shall see, this posture is adopted to hide the actual feint. The magician holds the coin with the tips of the fingers of his right hand, raising it to strike the palm of his left hand. On the first occasion, he completes this movement without making the coin vanish. On the second, or third strike, the coin is dropped from the raised hand into the space between neck and collar. If the movement is carried through without impediment, the audience will be convinced that the coin has been transferred to the left hand.

ESSENTIAL ITEMS

There are two accessories which are indispensible to the performing magician – a top hat and a wand, or walking stick. The deceptive nature of these will emerge as we examine tricks and illusions in which they are used. For example, I will reveal the most simple sleight with the hat in the next trick, and a variation on the standard wand is used in the trick on page 62.

~~~

The Top Hat Trick

The magician shows the audience that his top hat is empty. He pops it on the baize table in front of him, lifts it up, and proceeds to take object after object from the 'empty' hat. First comes a handkerchief, then some coloured ribbons, then a pair of large dice, some coins, and so on. Pretending that he has finished taking out objects, the conjurer turns over the hat – and out pops a small rabbit, or some other entertaining creature.

The rabbit as an afterthought is good entertainment. Among the few precepts left by Houdini as 'Helpful Hints for Young Magicians Under Eighty' was 'rabbit tricks are positive successes'. I am not sure how the rabbit feels, in the glare of the lights, but Houdini is right. Victorian conjurors, who were extremely fond of mechanical contrivances, even had special 'rabbit trap' doors built into some of their tables. This was a specially sprung port-hole into which a rabbit could be pushed, or from which it could be pulled, in the course of a magical entertainment.

HOW THE TRICK IS DONE

Given that it is possible to have a hidden hole through a table-top, and that there is some way of passing things through the top of the hat, then there is almost no limit to what may be taken from an 'empty' hat.

However, it is also quite remarkable what may be hidden in a conjurer's top hat, or even in a small hidden section of it. For instance, soft toys often look quite big but can be squeezed up and hidden inside a hat without much difficulty, which makes them ideal for trickery.

Also, what is supposed to be an empty hat may very well not be. Often, a hat may have a secret bottom, with a piece of white silk actually being a false lid. Although a false bottom is quite hidden from the audience, and perhaps only just over four centimetres deep, even so, it will hide many objects. For those who do not wish to resort to such mechanical trickery, this is how this classical hat trick is worked.

The top hat is indeed empty when the magician shows it to the audience. When he places it on the table in front of him, the brim slightly edges over the table. Below the table, yet within easy reach of the magician's grasp is a 'load', such as a large handkerchief, loosely tied into a bundle. This rests on a hidden table-ledge, which is at such a level as to permit the magician to grasp in his fingers the top of the handkerchief as he picks up the hat.

What the audience does not see, as the hat moves upwards in the magician's fingers, is that he has also taken up the bundle, and has managed to swing it into the hat. This is how the hat is loaded with goodies which may be taken out to the amazement of the audience. The magician must take the handkerchief out first, thus releasing the other objects into the hat. His rapid hand-movement in picking out the other objects usually keeps the rabbit in the bottom of the hat. However, if the rabbit does elect to reveal itself before the finale, all the the magician has to do is treat this as though it were part of the act – perhaps pretending that he had not expected to find a rabbit there at all.

One word of advice for amateur magicians – rabbits are unreliable performers. Experience has shown that it is far easier, and perhaps even more entertaining, to end the hat trick by producing a mechanical toy (already pre-wound) which is then allowed to run across the table.

A Hat and Wand Trick

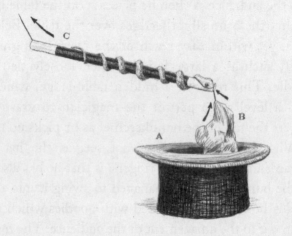

The magician shows a clown's conical hat to the audience, and establishes that it is quite empty. He drops into it a coloured handkerchief, or some other piece of cloth or silk.

Taking up a strange wand, which has a frog perched on the end, or perhaps a snake curled along the whole of its length, with its mouth open towards the end, the magician explains that this is no ordinary wand. The creature on it is a famous devourer of cloth. By way of demonstration, he plunges the frog or snake into the hat, and then pulls it out again. Now the magician reveals that the hat is quite empty and that the cloth has been gobbled up.

HOW THE TRICK IS DONE

The cloth is not devoured by the frog or snake, but by the wand, which is in fact a hollow tube. One corner of the handkerchief is tied with a cotton thread, which passes through the hollow wand. The thread continues up the sleeve of the magician, where it is anchored at the top.

"When the magician plunges the frog or snake into the hat, he stretches out his hand, which pulls at the thread. This action pulls the handkerchief, or cloth, into the hollow space inside the wand. When the wand is put down on the table, the magician breaks the thread, so as not to be impeded by it later.

Most magicians find that it is a good idea for their top hat and wand to be as ordinary as possible, since in one performance or another someone will probably demand to examine at least one of these closely. There can be few things more damaging to a performance than for a member of the audience to find secret pockets in a hat, or a false top to a wand. When this happens, the magic flies out of the window, and the audience may begin to yawn. Even so, top hats and wands are essential accessories, and it is a good idea to open a performance with the Top Hat trick described on page 59, if only because it involves the old-favourite rabbit taking his bow.

The standard wand, or stick, is not hollow, of course. In fact, the wand may be of a design unique to the magician, and may require no particular tampering with in terms of anticipated trickery. Today, an interesting range of 'ivory'-headed sticks is available. These have handles, or finials, in a variety of interesting designs made from methyl methacrylate, which gives the appearance of ivory.

∽

The Egg Dance

This original trick is a particular favourite with children. The magician produces half a dozen eggs, and places them on a table or on a top hat. He then borrows a stick, a cane, or something similar, from a member of the audience, and 'bewitches' this with magical passes. If one is not available from the audience, he produces his own, but permits the audience to examine it thoroughly before he uses it to perform the trick.

When the audience is satisfied that the stick is an ordinary one, albeit bewitched, the magician holds it over the eggs. If music is available, he then calls for this to be played. If not, he asks the audience to clap their hands 'to encourage the eggs'. At the sound of music, or clapping, one of the eggs begins to dance.

HOW THE TRICK IS DONE

The dancing egg has been pierced and blown in advance (see page 44) so that it is hollow. A long piece of dark cotton thread has been glued to the top or bottom of the egg. The other end of the thread has been tied around a crooked pin.

After the magician has borrowed the stick, and perhaps while he is bewitching it with secret passes 'known only to initiates', he contrives to stick the pin into his coat. The thread is either passed over the stick, or held in the same conjurer's hand as holds the stick. The slightest movement of the thread causes the egg to roll around, producing a knock-on effect so that the eggs around it move as well.

ℰⅩ𝒪

Using a Conjuring Table

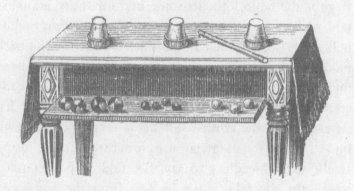

The majority of coin tricks are displays of leger-demain, and require few props, or gimmicks. Sometimes, however, a magician may find it better to work his or her tricks in front of a table which has specially designed secret shelves, drawers, and other hidden devices. The Top Hat trick on page 59 is a good example of the use of such a secret shelf, for carrying hidden items. The technical term for such shelves is 'servante', and the hidden objects upon it are the 'load'.

No doubt it is the sophistication of modern audiences which has discouraged this in recent years, yet the astute conjurer can become adroit at picking up objects from a servante in so casual a manner as not to draw the attention of the audience to his or her subterfuge. Sometimes, the servante is softly padded which enables the conjurer to drop small objects on it without making any tell-tale noises.

One related device occasionally used on the modern stage is the tablecloth. In some performances, an assistant will spread such a cloth over the magician's table, perhaps to suggest that its purpose is to make the trick more visible. In fact, one edge of the cloth has been folded over to form a natural pocket, which already contains objects required for the coming tricks. Alternatively, the cloth itself has a secret pocket sewn into it, which the magician uses for abstracting or losing small items. Needless to say, the fold or pocket must hang over the table edge hidden from the audience's view. When the cloth is cleared away by the magician's assistant (the magician having already moved on to another trick, thus diverting the attention of the audience), then so are the 'disappeared' objects.

Especially designed tablecloths are also used as a means of mystification. Sewn on to the surface of a sheet of coloured cloth are simple designs associated with the craft of the magician. These might be stars, flat representations of dice, and so on. One or two of these (usually located on the surface central to the table-top) are sewn in such a way as to act as pockets. Only a little dexterity is required to push coins into these pockets, in order to make them vanish from the sight of the audience. Very often, the table forms an intrinsic part of a deception; the following trick is quite stunning when performed well.

૭૪૭

A Table Trick

On the table is a cage, about the size of a bird-cage. The magician holds it up for everyone to see: he runs his fingers against the wire bars, as though strumming a harp, and taps the metal bottom, to show that it is solid. Then he places the cage back on the table.

The assistant carries on a box, from which she takes a rabbit. As she hands the rabbit to the magician, she briefly shows that the box is empty, by turning it upside-down. She puts the box to the back of the stage. The magician, or his assistant, then places the rabbit in the cage and drops a square of cotton fabric over it. When the magician pulls the fabric away a moment or two later, the rabbit has disappeared. His assistant walks over to the box at the back of the stage, and takes out the missing rabbit.

The great Victorian magician, Professor Hoffmann, illustrated a collapsible bird-cage of this kind which could not only make the rabbit, or bird, within it disappear, but which would even disappear itself.

HOW THE TRICK IS DONE

The top of the table has a secret hinged door, slightly smaller than the bottom of the cage. The bottom of the cage is also a hinged door, with a catch that is released from the top of the cage.

When the magician places the cloth over the cage, he presses the release button on top of the cage, the doors spring open downwards, and slide the rabbit into a partition (a 'load chamber') hidden beneath the table. The rabbit which is discovered later in the box is not the same as the one which has been vanished. The rabbit was in the box all the time, yet because the box has a false pocket, it was not seen when the first rabbit was extracted.

CHAPTER 3

SLEIGHTS WITH COINS AND SMALL OBJECTS

Most audiences expect a magician to be able to perform a few tricks with coins, or with small objects like rings and dice, and many amateurs try to include these in their repertoire. Coin tricks can sound like simplicity itself, especially when you know exactly how sleights are done, but they are very difficult to perform well. As with many other magical deceptions, the only way to succeed is to practise each trick until it feels like second nature to you. If you find palming a coin almost impossible at first, do not give up. Remember, too, that simple devices with which to vanish coins and small objects can be bought from magic shops and suppliers.

Tricks with Coins and Dice

Coin tricks are the essence of conjuring. An entertainer who cannot make a coin disappear and then reappear in a most unlikely place is scarcely a magician of any worth. The truth is that most coin tricks depend entirely upon nimble fingers for their effectiveness. The early 19th-century magician, Jules de Rovere, was so aware of this that he invented a new word to cover the manual dexterity behind such tricks. His word was based on what he imagined to be the Latin for 'quick fingers'. By merging 'presti' and 'digiti' (actually, a mix of Italian and Latin), de Rovere

gave us 'Prestidigitater'. This word was eagerly seized upon by magicians, anxious for high-flown titles with which to emblazon their advertisments and calling cards.

A good magician who has mastered the art of leger-demain may appear to do his tricks with ridiculous ease, yet his skill will have been acquired through years of assidious practice. Anyone who doubts this should try a little experiment. Hold up a coin, caught between your thumb and index finger. Now, let the coin drop, so that it falls into your hand. For the sake of this experiment, it does not matter whether it falls into your palm, or into the crook of your fingers. What you have to do is release the coin (by pulling back your thumb almost imperceptibly) without moving your other fingers, and without jerking your hand as a whole. Try this, and you will see how difficult such a sleight is. Remember that this is only the beginning of the most simple of all sleights practised in magical performances.

If this experiment proves to be too difficult, then have a go at palming a coin, in the manner described below. Try carrying a coin, palmed in your hand, for only 20 minutes, while you go around your ordinary daily business. This is not as easy as you might think, and at the end of the experiment, you will probably have a new respect for conjuration.

An amateur may be gifted as an entertainer, even as a magician, but there is only one route to an impressive repertoire of coin tricks – long practice. The remarkable Robert-Houdin did not mince his words when he remarked that the secret of success as a conjurer lay first in dexerity; second, in dexterity; and third, in dexterity. The magician Geoff Sharp performs the 'stacking dice' trick with remarkable dexterity. He places four dice in two rows in front of him, and with a rapid swinging motion catches each of the dice in turn (working down both rows at once), to finish with the four dice balancing on top of each other. As a delightful addition to this sleight of hand, Sharp can ask a member of the audience to say on which level of the four dice he or she would like to see a change of colour. Sharp seems to be the first magician to perfect the art of stacking two rows of dice in a single movement.

Fortunately for amateurs, there are one or two effective coin tricks which, while demanding some degree of dexterity, are less demanding than the sophisticated tricks offered by the great masters. First, however, here are a few of the basic techniques, gimmicks and supports used by conjurers to perform the majority of coin tricks.

For all the magician makes use of clothing and table-magic in his coin tricks, the real work is done with his hand. A large number of different sleights have been invented and described by magicians, but only two are recommended for amateurs. The first is usually called 'palming', a technique which was dubbed 'the very corner-stone of conjuring' by Professor Hoffmann.

Palming involves holding a coin between the top of the hypothenar eminence (the Mount of Moon, according to palmists), and on the lower part of the index finger. Provided that the entertainer does not show the front of his palm to the audience, his hand (albeit grasping the coin) may take hold of other objects, and perform most natural actions, as though nothing were in the palm at all. Anyone can learn how to hold a coin in this way, but it takes hours of practice. Some modern conjurers regard this sleight as awkward and old fashioned, and have developed other methods of hiding coins in their hands. The next trick involves one such sleight.

☙❧

The Vanishing Coin

The magician offers sight of a coin in his right hand. It is held between his thumb and index finger. He moves his left hand towards his right, and takes the coin. However, when he opens his left hand a moment later, the coin has vanished.

HOW THE TRICK IS DONE

The coin never leaves the right hand. In moving his left hand towards the right, he twists the index finger of his right hand over (thus, for a brief yet important moment hiding the coin from the sight of the audience). At this same moment, he releases the thumb's grip of the coin. At the same time, the two fingers carry the coin to the palming position shown on page 70. Naturally, this palming operation is not seen by the audience. What everyone thinks they see, however, is that the fingers have dropped the coin into the half-open left hand.

The magician separates his hands, and continues with the trick, while the audience is convinced that the coin is now in his left hand. When done properly, this palming action is totally convincing, but it is a sleight which requires considerable practice.

Palming is not a sleight used only in coin tricks – the technique may be used to dazzle audiences with the disappearance of any number of small objects, provided they are sufficiently small to be palmed in the hand without discomfort.

The number of tricks which require a degree of manual dexterity of this kind is probably endless. They range from the relatively simple displays of vanishing coins, to fairly complex trick sequences in which palming or similar techniques play only a small (though essential) part in the display. The next couple of effective and popular tricks demonstrate how such sleights are used.

❦

Transmuting a Large Coin

The magician borrows a large coin from a member of the audience. He places this in the middle of a square of paper, which he folds up, to make a square packet. He places this on a second square of paper, and folds this also into a packet. He places this on a third square of paper, and folds it to make another packet.

Now the magician taps the packet with his magic wand, utters some magic words, and unfolds all three sheets to reveal that the coin has changed into a much smaller one. The magician borrows a handkerchief and places the small coin beneath it. This is given to a member of the audience, who holds it over a glass of water. At a word from the magician, he or she releases the coin, which can be heard splashing into the water. When the handkerchief is removed, there is no coin in the glass. As the coin has been magicked away 'for ever', the magician takes another from his own pocket, and gives this to the original lender, so that he or she does not feel cheated.

HOW THE TRICK IS DONE

For the first part of the trick, the magician prepares four squares of paper. Two are about 10 cm x 10 cm (4 in x 4 in). One is slightly larger, and the fourth is larger still. One of the smallest pieces is folded at the top edge, to overlap about one-third down. The bottom edge is folded up so that it slightly overlaps this folded top edge. The other two sides are folded over, in a similar way.

The second small sheet is folded in exactly the same way. These two sheets are glued back to back, leaving the open folds facing outwards on either side. This small double packet is placed in the centre of a larger sheet of paper, and a similar series of four folds is made, to enclose the packet. The same thing is done with the larger sheet.

Once the folds have been made, the magician unfolds the outer sheets of paper, and undoes one side of the glued sheets. He secretly places a small coin inside one of the paper purses, and folds this up.

When the time comes to perform the trick, the magician shows the packet of papers to the audience, and opens them up. He borrows from the audience a large coin which he places on the open package, and folds over the first paper. With the pretence of showing that there is no trickery, he holds this up between his fingers towards the audience. This allows him to turn the package over when he places it back on the larger sheets. Now the large coin is underneath, and the packet with the hidden smaller coin is on top. The magician completes all the folds of the other sheets. After pronouncing the magic words, he unfolds the sheets to reveal that the large coin has been devalued to a smaller one.

It sometimes happens that someone in the audience insists on marking the original large coin, or making a note of its date. If this happens, the magician must act accordingly. After performing the handkerchief trick (explained below), he retrieves the 'lost' large coin by repeating the first trick. This time, however, he simply folds up the papers without placing a coin on the first sheet, and produces the large coin, which has remained inside the packet at the back of the pile all the time.

For the second part of the trick, using a handkerchief,

the magician needs to have bought a glass disk which is exactly the same size as the small coin. Such disks are available from magic shops.

At the point when the handkerchief trick is to be performed, the magician palms this disk in the third finger of his right hand, and substitutes this for the small coin. The participant thinks that he is handed the coin, but in fact he is holding the disk. When he releases it into the glass of water, everyone can hear the disk drop in. When the handkerchief is removed, however, the disk cannot be seen because its translucency ensures that it remains invisible in the water.

So long as the participant has returned to his or her seat, to complete the trick, the magician can pour the water into a jug and turn the glass upside-down, to show that it is empty. This is works because the wet disk will stick to the bottom of the glass, and will only be spotted by someone who is very near the magician.

༺༃༻

Identifying a Lady's Coin

The magician asks a woman in the audience to provide a large coin, which can be marked, if she so chooses. Alternatively, she can make a note of the date on the coin.

The magician has two other coins, which he holds up for the audience to see. Now, he invites a member of the audience to blindfold him. The three coins are placed and moved around on a baize table in front of the magician. He then touches each of the coins in turn, and unerringly picks out the one which belongs to the lady.

HOW THE TRICK IS DONE

This amusing deceit is simplicity itself. The magician has been gripping his own two coins tightly, so that they are very warm. The coin from the lady, on the other hand, is cold because she has taken it from her purse. Thus, the magician is able to distinguish the coins because of their different temperatures. This is why the magician asks a woman to give him the coin. The chances are that a coin offered from a man would come from his trouser pocket, and would also be warm. The trick is done on a baize table because the heat loss is not so dramatic as it would be on a good conductor, such as a plastic table-top, a ceramic tray, and so on.

The magician, David Devine, recorded an amusing account of how this trick (in his day called 'The Marked Shilling') almost went wrong. A garrulous gentleman in the audience accused him of nicking the edges of his own two coins, in order to be able to distinguish these from the one offered by the lady. Devine, while denying this, was at a loss for a moment, but then had the inspiration to ask the gentleman to produce his own two coins. These were duly taken from the gentleman's pocket, and placed on the table with the one from the lady's purse. The coin from the purse was cold but the coins fresh from the man's pocket were still warm, as Devine had expected them to be, and so he was still able to operate the trick effectively.

☙❧

The Weisenheimer Ring Trick

The magician takes a coloured plastic or metal ring, which looks like a small bangle or hoop, and holds it up to the audience for examination. Now he takes a coin, and puts it on the table. He picks up a ring, places it over the coin, and immediately covers the ring with a piece of card. The magician utters a few magic words, and lifts up the card to reveal that the coin has disappeared.

HOW THE TRICK IS DONE

The ring which is shown to the audience is not the same as the one used in the trick. The trick-ring has been specially prepared, prior to the entertainment. In the profession, this is called a Weisenheimer ring.

A circle of baize, exactly the same colour and texture of the baize on the table, has been glued in advance to

the bottom of the ring. The edge is carefully trimmed, so that there is no material sticking out. In this version, the trick is being worked on a red surface, so the middle of the ring has been filled with the same red fabric. When this ring is placed over a coin on the table, the circle of baize covers it. Since the inner circle of baize cannot be distinguished from the baize of the table, the coin is no longer visible.

In this trick, the coin actually 'disappears' before the sheet of card is placed over the ring. The card is a decoy, intended to suggest that the coin has disappeared only after the issue of a magic formula.

The principle behind the Weisenheimer ring trick has several extensions. For example, it is possible to treat the rim of a drinking glass in the same way as the ring. When the glass is placed over a coin, or other flat object, it will 'disappear'. Most magicians who use this form of the Weisenheimer make special cylindrical covers for their glasses (usually from card). This adds to the mystique, and also prevents over-zealous eyes seeing the false baize top of the glass.

A most effective, yet simple, extension of the Weisenheimer may be worked in connection with the Marvin trick described on page 85. A spare flat ring from the Marvin set is covered with baize, to perform the Weisenheimer. This is placed casually on the table while the original Marvin trick is being performed, and may be used to make individual coins vanish during the performance. This is one of two interesting tricks where the

Weisenheimer may be used as part of a more extensive trick. The next trick is another version.

℘

The Nine Coins Trick

On the table is a top hat, a tray, nine coins and a set of rings, among which are three Weisenheimer rings. The magician shows that the hat is empty. He places six of the coins on the tray, leaving three of the coins on the table-top. Then he tips the coins into the hat. He places the three Wiesenheimer rings over three of the coins on the table, covering these with a single handkerchief. Holding his magic wand over the handkerchief, he instructs the three coins to leap into the hat. He pulls away the handkerchief to show that the coins have vanished. Finally, the magician tips over the top hat with a dramatic flourish to reveal that all nine coins are inside it.

HOW THE TRICK IS DONE

The magic is worked because the tray has been specially constructed with a secret false bottom, which contains a shallow groove which holds a number of coins. You can buy such trays from magic shops. Before the trick is performed, the magician hides three coins in this hidden groove – in other words, unknown to the audience, there are 12 coins altogether.

To draw attention away from the tray, the top hat may be handed around for examination, before the trick is performed. People are naturally and justifiably suspicious of conjurers' top hats, so this is always a useful diverting ploy. It may be a good idea to hand out a couple of rings for examination as well, but not the Weisenheimers, of course. Also it is very important not to hand over the tray – luckily the audience is not likely to be suspicious of this.

∞

Professor Hoffmann's Intelligent Coin

On the table in front of the magician is a wine glass. This may be examined by a member of the audience. The glass is placed on a book by the magician, who explains that this is an insulator, intended to show there is no connection between the table and the glass itself.

The magician borrows from the audience a large coin, puts it in the glass, and makes a few magic passes over it. The purpose of the magic, he explains, is to imbue the coin with mystic intelligence. Satisfied that the magical coin is prepared, the magician asks it a question, such as 'Are you ready to answer questions?' At these words, the coin jumps into the air, and can be heard falling back into the wine glass. Now the magician asks it more questions, to which the coin responds with a single leap for 'Yes'. To indicate 'No', it remains motionless.

According to records, this was a most popular trick in Victorian magical entertainments, and private soirees. There is little doubt that this wide popularity was extended by the writings of Professor Hoffmann. He was really no professor, but he was one of the most influential magicians of the last century. Basing his writings on the brilliant work of the French magician, Robert-Houdin, he was the first to publish an account of how this extraordinary trick, which he named 'The Intelligent Five Franc Piece' could be worked by the 'Prestidigitateur'.

HOW THE TRICK IS DONE

Before the coin is dropped into the glass, the magician presses to it a blob of wax. This wax is then pressed against an invisible thread, which hangs down from the flies above the stage. It is the thread, pulled by a confederate, which animates the coin.

The book, far from being an insulator, plays a most important role in the trick, because it has been specially prepared. The lower end of the invisible thread is attached to the book by means of a bent pin inserted into the cover. This enables the confederate to pull on the string without danger of upsetting the glass. Only a slight movement is required to make the coin move in a most mysterious manner. Naturally, the wineglass must be fairly heavy for the trick to work effectively.

The small blob of wax is secreted on the edge of the book, and is thus readily available for the magician, who must cover his deft manipulations with his patter. At the end of the trick, the wax is scraped from the coin, which is returned to the original donor. The book is moved from the table by an assistant, in order to ensure that the thread does not become entangled in a later trick. Since the thread hangs from the flies, and depends for its invisibility on the fact that its colour merges with the curtains behind, the magician must remember not to place his own face between the thread and the curtains. He therefore performs the trick standing slightly to one side.

∝∾

Marvin's Dynamic Coins Trick

Among the commercial products which are available in magic shops, few are easier to manipulate, or so mysterious in their operation, than the coin trick designed and marketed by Marvin. In fact, a simple version of this trick was known in earlier times as 'The Sphinx Coin Trick', and was performed by the Walker brothers on the British stage. In its more sophisticated form, this trick is susceptible to many variations, but its simplest manifestations appear to the audience as follows.

The magician places a small pile of coins on the table. He shows the audience a small brass cup, with milled edges, and a brass ring slightly smaller than the cup. To show that it is a genuine ring, the conjurer pushes his finger through the hole. If requested, he will happily allow a member of the audience to examine the cup and ring.

The magician places the brass cup over the pile of coins, and taps the top of the cup with his magic wand. When he lifts it, the coins have vanished. He takes the same empty brass cup, and places it over the brass ring. Again he taps the top of the cup with his wand. When he lifts the cup and ring, the coins have reappeared.

The magician may continue to perform a wide variety of similar vanishing and disappearing tricks with the aid of two or three of these brass cups and rings. Here are a number of such tricks.

The conjurer places the cup over the coins. He introduces a second ring and cup, which (again) he permits a member of the audience to examine. He places this second pair next to the third set. The coins are still hidden beneath the first cup – indeed, the magician may even lift this, to show that they are still there. After a few passes and magic words, he asks a member of the audience to point out under which cup the coins are placed. Naturally, the sharp-eyed participant points to the first set. The conjurer lifts this – to reveal that the coins have vanished.

With a knowing smile, the magician taps the top of the second ring and cup, lifts them, and shows that the coins have migrated magically to this position.

If the magician chooses to introduce three sets of cups and rings, then it possible for him to duplicate at will, and with the greatest ease, the mesmeric effect of the 'Three Ball Trick', which takes so much effort to practise well.

Using both hands, the magician places the pile of coins on top of an inverted cup. He places a second cup over this pile of coins, and picks up the entire set between his thumb and middle finger. He spins the whole assembly on the table surface, as though it were a top. The parts separate under the pressure of movement and reveal that the coins have disappeared. The magician hands the empty cups to someone in the audience for examination.

As the participant is walking away, to the appreciative applause of the audience, the magician calls him back, and asks if he would mind looking in his left pocket. Much to his embarrassment, the participant finds in this pocket a pile of coins. The conjurer presents these to him, as a parting gift, insisting that there was really no need to steal them.

HOW THE TRICK IS DONE

The effectiveness of the trick rests entirely on the cunning design of the cups and rings. Save for the top coin, the stack of coins is false. This means that when the stack is held inside the brass cup, it is invisible to the audience: the hollow inside of the coin-stack is taken by those watching to be the inside of the cup.

The trick depends upon the elasticity of the cups. The sides of each cup are specially sprung, and will hold the false stack of coins firmly in place, when a delicate pressure is applied to the top of the cup. The false stack will fall out (and once again look like a pile of coins) only when the cup has been placed on the ring, and its top tapped sharply. This sharp tap is sufficient to release the tension in the sides of the cup, and release the false stack.

When the magician wants to make the stack of coins disappear, he takes an empty cup by gripping the bevelled edge between his thumb and middle finger. He places the cup over the top of the stack of coins. With his index finger, he presses slightly upon the centre of the cup top. This is done in an unobtrusive manner, so that the audience is not aware that this is an essential part of the trick.

As he presses down, the magician feels the elastic movement of the brass. There is an almost imperceptible release of pressure, which confirms that the coins have been gripped. He lifts the cup to show to the audience that the coins have disappeared. It is important to note that the coins cannot be made to disappear (that is, be gripped by the cup) while the ring is underneath the cup.

In order to ensure that the trick is effective, the designers of cups have permitted sufficient space for a coin to be inserted on top of the false stack. When a coin is placed on top of the stack, this will be picked up, along, with the stack, when the top of the cup is pressed. The stacks are designed to take a current British ten pence piece. When this coin is used, the fit is so perfect that, even when the stacked cup is shaken, it makes no rattling sound, to give away the trick. An American quarter (25 cents), which, to all intents and purposes, is the same size as the tenpenny piece is actually slightly thinner, and of an almost imperceptibly smaller diameter. This means that if a quarter is used, the captured stack will rattle slightly when it is shaken, so you need to bear this in mind if performing the trick with an American coin.

When the magician wants to make the stack of coins appear, as through from within the empty cup, he makes sure that the stack of coins is hidden inside the cup. He takes the bevelled edge of the cup between his thumb and middle finger and shows the inside of this to the audience, to prove that it is empty. He then slips the cup over the brass ring, so as to grip both between thumb and middle finger.

Still holding the cup and ring in the same manner, he bangs these on the table-top with sufficient force to dislodge the 'coins'. If you decide to perform these tricks yourself, then, long before facing your public, you must learn to identify the precise feeling of the minimum shock required to dislodge the coins. In the finale to the trick described above, the conjurer simply plants the coins on the participant as the performance draws to a close.

The following notes should help you to perform the tricks more convincingly:

When you show the items to members of the audience, before the trick, it is a good idea to ensure that each object is handed to a separate member of the audience in turn. If the three are held by one person, it is possible that the trick might be worked out by accident. No matter how many stacks of coins you carry in secret, or use in the trick, the audience should be aware only of the existence of one stack of coins.

Always ensure that the audience sees that the cups are empty before making the coins appear. The tricks depend upon the elasticity of the cups, and it requires a fair amount of practice to learn the right pressures to grip and release the coins. When banging a set on the table (to release the coins), do not be too obvious, otherwise the audience may realize what is happening. This is one move which must be practised until you have it just right. You may find it practical to demonstrate the trick on a baize table-top, because this will deaden the sound, without significantly weakening the requisite shock.

Equally, when you plan to make the coins vanish, do not press the cup down too firmly. If you do this, the coins will not fall out with sufficient ease when the time comes to release them. Only practice will enable you to establish the correct pressure. You must remember that the audience (and especially any children in the audience) will be intent on trying to see how the trick is worked. Any seeming change in the movement of your hand (even in muscular flexion) will give the game away.

Commercial versions of this trick are sold with useful pamphlets describing several of the tricks which may be worked by means of cups, rings and coins.

✿

Hiding a Ring or a Coin in an Egg

This trick is a messy but entertaining one. The magician borrows a coin or a ring from a member of the audience. If it is a ring, he insists that it should not be a valuable one, as there is some danger in the trick, and the ring might be lost or damaged. When a coin or ring has been obtained, the magician hands around an ordinary raw egg for the audience to examine. Meanwhile, the coin or ring is vanished by the magician.

When the egg has been given back to the magician, he places it in an egg-cup, and asks his assistant or a member of the audience to slice off the top of the egg with a knife. Then she is encouraged to probe around in the egg to find the 'lost' coin or ring.

HOW THE TRICK IS DONE

The secret rests in the design of the egg-cup. In the bottom of the cup is a specially cut vertical indentation. When a coin or ring is dropped into the cup, it always slides into this groove, and comes to rest in a partly – or even completely – vertical position. Thus, when the coin or ring is pushed down on top of it, the object is forced through the bottom of the shell into the egg itself.

When the magician vanishes the coin or ring, in reality he palms it and transfers it to the egg-cup before he places the egg in it. In this way, the object is 'in' the egg before the top is sliced off.

If a ring is to be used, it must be suitable for the trick. This is why the magician issues a warning that the ring might be damaged. It is most unlikely to be harmed, of course, but it is important that the magician is able to select a ring with a small jewel-mount, which will fit into the groove inside the egg-cup. If the ring has too large a mount, it can be rejected on the grounds that it looks too valuable.

ℭℵℭ

Passing a Ring Through Matter

The magician borrows a ring from a member of the audience, and magnetizes this with several passes. While doing so, he explains to the audience that these passes are necessary in order to give the ring the power to pass through matter – at least, through wood and glass.

The magician holds up a black handkerchief to the audience, to show that it is empty. He places the ring in its folds, screws up the handkerchief, and hands it to a member of the audience, to hold. The person is asked to grip the ring through the cloth, to make sure that it does not disappear until the appropriate time.

Next, the magician hands around a large box, so that the audience may ensure that it is empty. When all and sundry are satisfied, the box is placed under the stage table, immediately below an empty glass, which rests upright on top of the table. The magician takes the hand-kerchief and, holding it by the ring, mutters a little magical mumbo jumbo to ensure that the magic will work. After a final magical pass, the ring is heard falling into the glass. Instead of remaining in the glass, however, it falls through the glass bottom, through the table-top, and into the box beneath the table.

The magician displays the handkerchief to show that the ring has indeed disappeared. He then asks his assistant to fetch the box from under the table. There is no doubt that the ring has penetrated glass and wood, for it is in the box.

HOW THE TRICK IS DONE

The magician has prepared a handkerchief and ring prior to the act. The ring is sewn to the handkerchief in such a way that when the latter is held out to the audience, the ring hangs down the back, unseen. This handkerchief and ring is the one held by the member of the audience. It is the same as is later dangled above the empty glass, and allowed to fall therein. The original 'magnetized' ring is palmed by the magician, and plays no part in the initial mumbo jumbo.

With the usual issue of magic words, the magician allows his own ring to fall into the glass, from the handkerchief. The audience hears it fall into the glass. However, when the black handerchief is removed, the magician ensures that the ring is carried up with it, leaving the glass empty.

Duped in this way, the audience is convinced that the original ring has penetrated the glass and table, to make its way to the box, as the magician claimed it would.

The original ring is found in the box because the magician puts it there. He palms the ring at the beginning of the trick, and pops it in the box when he places it under the table.

❧

The Three Balls Trick

This trick is a version of one recorded in the earliest collection of magical tricks published in England, *A Discovery of Witchcraft* by Reginald Scot. This is a general examination of conjuring tricks which were often confused with deeds of witchcraft. The book did much to popularize the conjurer's art and, by revealing certain of the entertainers' secrets, absolved them of the superstition of being witches.

To perform the trick, the magician takes up a long string, upon which three coloured balls, or heads, are threaded. He moves the balls around on the string, and swings the string lightly in the air to show that the balls, though threaded, are loose.

Leaving the ends of the string hanging, the magician covers the balls with a handkerchief. He invites two members of the audience to hold the ends of the string, to ensure that there is no trickery. On his command, the two pull gently at their respective ends. The string pulls away from beneath the handkerchief, leaving the three balls on the table. The string appears to have cut through the balls, without damaging them. The magician hands the balls to the audience to prove that they are still intact.

HOW THE TRICK IS DONE

Even before the performance begins, there are two pieces of string. The holes in two of the balls are of a sufficient diameter to take one string only. The hole of the third ball is just wide enough to take two strings. One of the two smaller-holed beads is threaded on the end of one string, while the other of the two is threaded on the end of the other string. The two ends of the strings are then inserted into the ball with the larger hole, one from either end, so as to overlap in the centre of the ball. The grip exerted by the middle ball on the string is sufficient to allow the conjurer to toss the balls up and down, and give the impression of their being on one complete string. However, when the two far ends of the strings are pulled against each other, the two middle ends are pulled from the central ball, and the three balls fall away.

One of the reasons the magician hands the balls to the spectators is to misdirect their attention from the string. The magician deftly picks up the two end pieces, and holds these severed ends in his hand, to give the impression that there is just one single string. He might also secretly take the opportunity to exchange the two pieces of string for a single piece of the same length, just in case someone asks to see this, as well as the balls.

❦

The Astral Box

A magic box stands on the conjuring table. The magician pats it fondly, and explains to the audience that it is an astral box, which permits material objects to disassemble its molecules, and fade into the astral plane – in other words, to vanish. While speaking, he opens the lid and tips the box forward to show that it is empty at the moment.

Next, the magician asks someone in the audience to lend him any small object – a watch, a pen, a handkerchief – in fact, anything which he or she cares to offer. He makes just two conditions. One, that the object should be small enough to fit in the magic box, and two, that, should the molecules not rearrange themselves properly, the owner should not mind if his or her possession is lost forever 'on the astral plane'.

The object is placed in the box, and the magician waves his magic wand. He may even recite a few magic words to complete the disappearing act. In any event, when he opens the box, and tips it forward, the object has disappeared.

All is not lost, however. After a few more words of mumbo jumbo and passes, the magician invites a member of the audience to open the box. Much to the mystification of the audience, the object is in the box once more, 'being lately returned from the vast spaces of the astral plane'.

HOW THE TRICK IS DONE

This is probably the oldest – and is certainly one of the simplest – disappearing tricks in the conjurer's book. In the profession, it is not called an astral box, but a 'changing box'. The best of the changing boxes are highly decorative, often with multi-coloured painted images. The magician might work part of the decoration into his patter, declaring for instance that a creature is the astral agent which ensures that the magic works.

Whatever its outer form, the box has hinged lids, cushioned in velvet, at its top and bottom. Inside, the box is divided by a diagonal partition, but because the inside is painted black, the casual observer would, on looking into it, imagine it to be an ordinary box.

When the magician wants to 'lose' an object, he puts it in one side of the box, and then contrives to turn the box over so that he can open the other lid. The lids are cushioned in order to silence the fall of the objects within as the box is turned over. At the turn, however, the magician ensures that his patter is in full swing. Although the box may be used for simple vanishing tricks, as set out above, as the professional name suggests, its real purpose is to effect a transformation or change of colour, or substance.

To do this, the magician needs to set up the tricks in advance, and not borrow something from the audience. For instance, he might change a red scarf to a green one, or a quantity of white sugar to red sand, and so on.

CHAPTER 4

PERFORMING WITH PLAYING CARDS

Experienced magicians are expected to be able to make coins and small objects vanish and reappear at a wave of a magic wand. Similarly, most performers will include a few playing card tricks in an entertainment – with the aim of baffling onlookers. Audiences like to be involved, even if they are just being asked to pick a card, and participants nearly always try to catch out the magician and see how a trick is done. For this reason, it is best to resist performing card tricks until you feel totally confident. Once again, the only way to carry off tricks with style is to spend hours practising until you are in complete control and feel at ease with the cards.

Simple Card Tricks

Now that you know how to do simple coin sleights, here are some with playing cards. The art of performing quality card tricks demands the greatest degree of practice imaginable. Anyone who has watched a master at work will be aware of just how extraordinary such tricks may be. The practised magician can force any card, without having to resort to using specially designed force packs (see Glossary, page 225). This means that to all intents and purposes he or she can completely control the fall of cards during a trick. Such finesse is only earned at a great price and it takes years for an amateur to become an accomplished entertainer with a pack of cards.

Fortunately, there are a number of tricks with cards which do not call for such sophisticated and professional skills. The only deceit which an amateur performer is likely to require is what is called the 'force'.

Forcing a card is a trick whereby a person (usually a member of the audience) is induced to take a particular card, or set of cards, when he or she believes that a free choice is being made. The notion behind such forcing is that the participant thinks that he or she is the only one to know what the card is – unless of course, the card is shown to others. In fact, the truth is that the magician also knows the identity of the card. Indeed, even before the trick is begun, the magician usually decides the identity of the card which he will eventually force upon the participant, and he will have arranged some of his tricks with this in mind.

Each of the next five tricks depends upon a forced card. The first is the simplest trick, and those which follow are more complex developments – in a sense, more dramatic presentations – of the fact that the magician knows, in advance of performing the trick, which card will be selected by the participant. Since the magician knows what the card will be, he can exercise all his ingenuity to reveal this card to the audience in some unexpected, entertaining or puzzling way.

The five tricks show how a basic idea can be given increasingly dramatic presentation. The first trick involves a couple of the secrets of forcing single cards, or small groups of cards. The second trick requires the use of a simple houlette, a mechanical device for making a forced card appear, as though by magic. In the third trick, a missing card is revealed from inside a melon. In the fourth trick, the magician throws a whole deck of cards into the air, and his assistant catches the forced card on a bat. And finally, in the most complex and entertaining of the variants on this theme, the chosen card is shot from a gun onto an ordinary tennis bat where it is pinned to the bat by the projected bullet, or missile fired.

༄

Forcing a Playing Card

Accomplished magicians can usually force any card by means of pure sleight of hand. However, special packs of cards have been developed to help an amateur to force a card, and it is easiest to begin forcing with the aid of a special forcing pack. These can be bought from magic shops – several different types are available commercially.

By far the simplest forcing pack consists of 51 cards of the same designation, plus one different card. This is kept on top, and is intended to suggest to the casual observer that all the cards in the pack are different.

An ideal forcing pack is the Svengali Deck (which is described in more detail in the Glossary, see page 231), in which alternate cards are identical. Most commercially available Svengali packs are accompanied by useful literature on how to work a variety of convincing tricks based on forcing. Another forcing pack is known as the 'Bank of Three', which is used in the Three Mysterious Cards trick. It is difficult to describe a specific forcing trick, because it depends on which cards are in the forcing pack.

However, this is a simple example of how a magician might perform a trick – there is an almost infinite number of permutations. Many can be most dramatic, but ultimately it depends on the magician's familiarity with the various methods of forcing.

The magician offers a pack of cards to a member of the audience, and asks him or her to select a card at random. The chosen card may be shown to the audience at large, but not to the magician, who should not see that, in this case, for instance, it is the Queen of Hearts. The card is returned to the pack, which is then shuffled, and placed in a box on the table.

The magician takes from the same table a sealed envelope. He hands this to another member of the audience, and instructs him or her to open it. Inside the envelope is the Queen of Hearts.

HOW THE TRICK IS DONE

The trick works because the audience believes that the card in the envelope is is the same Queen of Hearts which was chosen from the pack. However, this is not the case. It is a second Queen of Hearts, placed in the envelope in advance by the magician, who is confident that he will be able to force the member of the audience to select this particular card.

ↂ

The Three Mysterious Cards

The magician places two packs of cards on the table. He takes one pack, and fans it for the audience to see. He throws all the cards into a hat, and asks his assistant to take out any three. As she removes them, she places them, one by one, in an envelope. Having completed the draw, she places the envelope on the table – perhaps on a card rack, so that it is upright, and visible to the audience.

The magician takes the other pack of cards from the table. He fans them (face downwards), and asks three individual members of the audience to select one card each, at random. The participants then hand these three cards in turn to the assistant. As she receives them, she calls out what they are, and places them on the table or card rack, next to the envelope.

When the triple draw is completed, the assistant opens the envelope, and takes out the cards one by one. The three cards in the envelope are identical to those which were selected by the three members of the audience.

HOW THE TRICK IS DONE

This traditional forcing entertainment is a variant on a parlour trick which was very popular with conjurers in the 1930s. Only one of the two packs is a standard pack with 52 different cards, but even this has been slightly tampered with. Before the trick has begun – and unknown to the audience – three cards are pinned together with a paper clip. When fanning the cards, and handling them subsequently, the magician keeps his finger over the clip, to hide it from the audience. The identity of the three cards is determined by the particular nature of the other pack. For the purpose of this present example, they are the Ten of Diamonds, Queen of Spades and Two of Hearts.

When the magician showers this pack of cards into his 'magic' hat, these are kept together. The assistant feels for the paper clip inside the hat and pulls out the three chosen cards, secretly removing the paper clip before she puts the cards in the envelope. In fact, it is good theatre-magic to have someone from the audience take these cards from her, and place them in the envelope, to convince those watching that there is no trickery afoot.

The second deck is far from ordinary – it is a forcing pack known as a 'Bank of Three'. In effect, it is possible to choose only four different cards from the pack. For the sake of this trick, imagine that there are 17 identical Ten of Diamonds, 17 Queen of Spades and 17 Two of Hearts, plus one other card to make up the 52. Each type of card is grouped together in sequence within the pack – all the Queens are together, and so on.

The magician offers the fanned set to three different members of the audience, ensuring each time that the relevant arc of cards is fanned in order to force each of the three different cards. To force the Ten of Diamonds, he fans out these 17 cards, keeping the others packed together in his left hand. When he moves to the next spectator, he moves this batch over to his right hand, and fans out the next 17 cards in the middle of the pack (in this case, the Queen of Spades). When this card has been forced, he moves to the next spectator, and fans out the remaining 17 cards, holding all the others in his right hand.

This devious way of presenting the cards may seem to be rather obvious, but the sleight always works. Generally speaking, people are quite prepared to take the card which is nearest to them, or easiest to reach – it is largely on this knowledge that the trick of forcing is based. The rest is pure theatre. As the magician knew all along which three cards would be in the envelope, and which three cards would be selected by the audience, he can build in as much patter and side-entertainment as he thinks fit.

It is possible to perform a less impressive version of this trick with only one card being picked from the hat, and a duplicate being forced on the audience. In this case, the forcing can be done with the aid of a Svengali Deck, and a participant may be allowed to cut the pack.

❧

The Rising Card

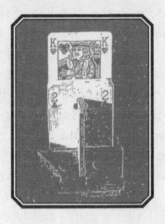

The magician invites a member of the audience to select a card – any card – and show it to those around him or her. Only the magician must not know the identity of the card. The chosen card is returned to the pack, which is well shuffled.

The magician or his assistant places the pack in a houlette on a table. The pack remains visible to the audience, but is not within the magician's reach.

The magician or his assistant rings a bell, at the sound of which a card mysteriously rises in the houlette, without any visible agency operating it. The rising card is the one which was originally chosen by the member of the audience.

HOW THE TRICK IS DONE

This is the classic forced card trick, and its extraordinary effect depends on the mystery of how the card rises. This has nothing to do with the sounding of the bell but solely depends on the peculiar construction of the houlette. Some houlettes are very complex, while others may be designed to entertain. One or two magicians have a houlette in the form of a small altar, with an idol seated beyond it; they delight in giving the impression that it is the pagan idol which makes the card to rise. But the idol is optional – a teddy bear or nothing would do just as well.

The magician knows in advance which card he is going to force. Accordingly, he has placed an identical card in a special rising card pack (see Glossary, page 230). In short, this is a set of cards which has had a rectangle cut from the bases of all but three of the cards. Two of the uncut cards are placed at the front and back of the set, to give the audience the impression that the pack is untampered with. The third card is identical to the card which is to be forced. The magician switches the original pack with this rising card pack, and it is this which is placed in the houlette.

The houlette has been prepared in such a way that a piece of cotton stretches about 2 cm (¾ in) along its bottom. When the string is loose, the cards are sufficiently heavy to weight it down. When the string is pulled taut, the cards will be lifted by the string. However, those cards which have been especially cut at their base will not be lifted at all.

In theory, the three whole cards (those uncut) should be lifted. However, as the magician wants only the forced card to rise, he has made special provision for these two cards. If he is a skilled magician, he will palm them both, and dispose of them in the course of the trick, so that they play no further part in the performance.

If he is not so skilled, the magician will have adapted the houlette to take the two unwanted cards into account. In this case, the string of cotton will not run right across the bottom of the houlette. Instead it runs from an upright needle, which has been inserted about 5mm (¼in) from the outer edge of the houlette. This means that there is a space which is not subject to the rising effect of the taut cotton string. The magician ensures that when he is placing the cards into the pack, the two whole end cards are dropped among the first few cards, into the space of the houlette which is free of the string. Although it does not matter if a single card is speared on the needle point, a little practice will enable the magician to drop the cards in without damaging them. When correctly placed, only the card intended to rise will be resting on the string.

The string is pulled taut by the magician. When he rings the bell, he pushes the houlette slightly forward on the table. The string is tied to the far side of the table, and therefore tightens as a result of this slight movement. The ring of the bell is merely a decoy to hide this action.

When the trick is over, the houlette is lifted casually from the table and placed on a chair or similar support behind. This is to prevent the magician from being caught up in the cotton as he continues his act. Alternatively, he can contrive to break the cotton so that it does not get in the way.

❧

Finding a Card in a Melon

The magician invites a member of the audience to select a card and show it to everyone except the magician. The chosen card is placed back in the pack, which is well shuffled.

The magician selects a large melon from a basket of fruit on the table and picks up a small kitchen knife. With this, he cuts the melon – making a deep slit. When he pulls out the knife, a portion of the chosen card can be seen stuck on the blade.

HOW THE TRICK IS DONE

The original card is forced. Before he performs the trick, the magician cuts the designated card to the same shape as the knife blade, and sticks this lightly on to the blade with a dab of glue. Over this, he slips a thin piece of sheet metal, or mirror paper, cut to the same shape as the blade. This protective surface cuts into the fruit, but it is left in the melon when the knife is withdrawn. It is important that the magician does not cut right through the melon. He stops half-way, when the entire blade of the knife is covered, so that it is possible to withdraw the blade, and leave its false covering hidden inside the fruit. All evidence of the deceit is left within the melon.

✍

The Magic Bat

The magician allows a member of the audience to choose a card from a pack. The card is shown to the audience (but not to the magician), and then returned to the pack which the magician shuffles well.

The magician's assistant picks up an ordinary cricket bat and swings it around, as though for practice. The magician throws the pack of cards into the air and, as they scatter, the assistant takes a swipe at them. To the amazement of the audience, the selected card is found stuck to the front of the bat.

HOW THE TRICK IS DONE

This effective trick is simple to perform, yet almost always stunning in its reception. There are several ways of ensuring

113

that the forced card is found on the bat. The following is one very simple method. The next trick, with the Magic Table Tennis Bat, gives an alternative, and perhaps more elegant, solution.

The magician forces the card on the audience. The deck which is thrown into the air is an ordinary pack.

Before the performance, a duplicate of the forced card is prepared. First, its back is painted black, so that it cannot be seen against the black background. Next the back is coated liberally with spray glue, and its front is lightly sprayed with it. Then the card is hung in a convenient position, on two invisible strings which run taut from the ceiling (or from the flies above the stage) to the floor. The front of the card is stuck to these strings in such a position that the assistant can swing the front of the bat towards the card, and catch it so that the back of the card sticks to the bat's striking edge. This is done immediately before the magician throws the cards into the air, as part of the final swing by which the forced card is 'caught' from the flying pack.

This is a simple way of ensuring that the right card is caught on the bat. Other stratagems include having a special cover, the same colour as the bat. This rests over the card, and is slid down at the appropriate moment by means of a cotton thread, pulled by the assistant. This device, while effective during a stage performance, where the audience is some distance from the bat, is impossible in a more intimate situation.

❧

The Magic Table Tennis Bat

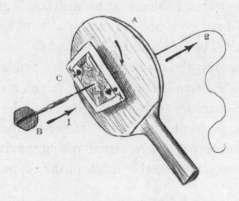

This is perhaps the most effective card trick which may be performed without any special skill. Although not so sophisticated as the shooting acts of great magicians such as Chung Ling Soo (the stage name of an American, William E. Robinson), it has almost the same electrifying effect on an audience.

The magician asks a member of the audience to pick a card from a pack. The card is shown to the audience (but not to the magician), and then returned to the deck, which is well shuffled by the magician. He then places the pack on the table.

Apparently forgetful of the cards, the magician sets up a target on the far side of the room. He takes a bow and arrow, or a gun which shoots small suction darts, and shoots at the target, to show that he is an excellent marksman. Then he asks everyone if they saw the movement of the dart in its flight, knowing that it would have been too rapid for them to follow it exactly. He continues with his patter, explaining that his assistant is gifted with especially sharp eyes. She is not only able to see the dart move, but will be able to catch it in flight.

As he speaks, the magician hands his assistant a table tennis bat. She stands fairly near the target, awaiting the shot. The magician takes aim, fires, and his assistant catches the projectile on the bat. However, the projectile has also, quite mysteriously, carried with it the chosen card, which is now pinned to the paddle of the bat by the dart.

HOW THE TRICK IS DONE

The card is forced and an identical card has been prepared in advance. A thin black thread has been tied through the centre of the arrow or dart. The same thread passes through a hole in the centre of the card, and then through the paddle of the bat. The end of the thread is tied to stage furniture – perhaps a table or chair -behind the assistant.

When the assistant takes a swipe at the imagined arrow or dart, the string is pulled taut. There is no arrow or dart to catch, for on this occasion, the magician shoots a blank. As soon as the loose string is pulled taut, the projectile tied to its end slams over the card, which is also pulled into the bat. The effect is that the dart and card stick to the paddle of the bat, giving the audience the impression that they have both been arrested in mid-flight. The card will be held in place if the paddle of the bat has been lightly covered with spray glue.

The string is pulled taut by the assistant when she swipes at the 'bullet'; the thread passes through the hole in the bat, and the paddle of the bat slams against card and dart. It does not matter if the movement of the swipe is so strong that it breaks the thread, because the card will stick to the glue on the paddle of the bat.

Some rehearsal is needed to perform the trick effectively. Since it is easiest to work the trick if the card and dart lie on the floor in front of the batting assistant, it is a good idea to hide these objects behind some stage furniture. To this end, before embarking on the trick, the magician may carry on a sport's bag, from which he takes the bow or gun, the projectiles, the bat, and so on. If he casually leaves the bag on the floor, and drops the strung dart and card behind it, they will remain hidden from the audience's view.

✆

Naming a Sequence of Cards

The magician invites a member of the audience on stage. He hands him or her a pack of cards, and makes an astounding claim. He says that, merely by weighing individual cards, he can distinguish and identify them. His fingers, he insists, are extremely sensitive to the weights of numbers, colours and shapes.

The guest is invited to shuffle the pack thoroughly. The magician shows how this trick was done in former times, and explains that earlier magicians usually had to cheat because they did not have such sensitive fingers. The magician takes the pack and places it on the table. He asks a member of the audience to do a final cut in front of everyone, and then takes the top card, which he weighs on his forefinger. Then he announces, after a little hesitation – pretending that he is finding the answer difficult – 'This card is a number card … Yes, it is a … an eight. It has the weight of a red card. Yes, my sensitive fingers tell me that … it is a heart. This card is the Eight of Hearts.' Thus, taking a number of cards from the pack in turn, he weighs them, and identifies them correctly, much to the astonishment of the audience.

HOW THE TRICK IS DONE

The pack which is shuffled is not the same as the pack which is laid on the table. After shuffling the first pack, the magician secretly swaps this with a second one. The cards in this second pack have been pre-arranged in a particular order, as follows.

First, all the suits are separated. Each suit is set out in its own pile, in the following order:

♥ HEARTS　♦ DIAMONDS
♣ CLUBS　♠ SPADES

These are then spread out, so that each of the 52 cards is visible.

In turn, the magician selects cards from each of the four suits in this order:

Thus, he takes the Eight of Hearts, which he places this face-upwards in front of him. On top of this he places the King of Diamonds, also face-upwards. He follows this with the Three of Clubs, then the Ten of Spades. All 52 cards in the pack are arranged in this way. The magician has to memorize this order, which he does with the aid of a simple mnemonic:

Anyone who wants to perform this trick need only learn the mnemonic, and remember the order of the cards in the four suites. After the rigmarole of the shuffling of the first pack, the magician dispenses with these, substituting the prepared pack.

Knowing the order of the cards, the magician hands this prepared pack to a member of the audience, and asks him or her to make a final cut. After this single cut has been made, the magician selects the top card, and balances it on his finger, as though to weigh it – he does not in fact know the identity of this card. In order to find out what it is, he demonstrates to the audience the way in which the trick was practised in former times. He balances it on his finger, and holds it slightly higher than his eye level. 'This,' he says, 'is how the trick was done formerly.' As he speaks, the magician can actually identify the card because he can see it, but he continues, 'Naturally, this crude deceit was easily detected, and I have no intention of attempting to fool an intelligent audience like you in such a way. I am not going to use trickery. Instead, I shall balance the cards at my waist, and identify the cards purely by their weight.' By this stratagem, the magician has identified the card, and therefore knows the sequence of the whole pack. For instance, if the card is the Ten of Clubs, the magician knows that the next card in the pack is the Two of Spades. He can then proceed to astound, as he claims, without resorting to any more deceit.

∽⚬∿

Finding the Lady

The magician hands a pack of cards to a member of the audience, and asks him or her to deal these out until he comes to a Queen – it does not matter which suit.

When a Queen is located, the remainder of the pack is discarded. The Queen is mingled with the cards dealt so far, and shuffled by the member of the audience, who hands the pack back. The magician shuffles the cards, and then deals these out into three rows. He asks a member of the audience to choose a row. Next the magician takes this row, and places it aside. He asks another member of the audience to choose a second row. He takes this, and places it alongside the first set. Only one row remains. He takes this up, and asks how many he should deal out before revealing the Queen. If the audience shouts 'Six', he deals out six cards. The seventh card is the Queen.

HOW THE TRICK IS DONE

The secret to this baffling trick is that the magician knows all along which card is the Queen. All four Queens in the original pack have been specially prepared, so that they are tapered. Although this tapering is so subtle that a member of the audience would not spot it, the magician knows exactly which cards are Queens when he handles the pack.

Before he deals out the cards for the first time, the magician ensures that the first of the Queens is about a third of the way down the pack. This is necessary to allow at least 15 cards to fall on the table during the deal. When this set of 15 or so cards has been re-dealt into three rows, the magician knows in which row the card is placed.

It does not matter which of the rows is selected by the audience. If the first row chosen contains the Queen, the magician simply proceeds with the trick, as though that had been his intention all along. He takes up this row, and asks how many he should deal out, before dealing the card.

If the second row chosen contains the Queen, he gathers this up, and places it on top of the stack made by the first row. He gathers the third row, and places this at the bottom. The Queen is now somewhere near the top, in the first five or six cards. If the third row contains the Queen, the magician merely picks this up, giving the impression that his intention all along was to eliminate the other two rows. So, whichever row contains the Queen, the magician proceeds with the trick.

Since the magician knows which card is the Queen, he can deal it from the stack at any chosen moment. If the audience asks for six cards, and the card is the seventh, he slips one of the cards during the deal. If the card is near the top, he simply underdeals, until the appropriate moment. For all its simplicity, this is a bewildering trick for the audience, which sees it as an example of mind-reading.

CHAPTER 5

FROGS, SPIDERS AND OTHER CREATURES

Whether or not a magician performs with live creatures depends largely on his attitude, and what the trick involves. Although animals and birds undoubtedly must have suffered in the hands of past magicians, today there is no need for any cruelty to be involved. For instance, a trick can be just as entertaining if a live creature is substituted with a model or fake version – it is easy to find realistic or humorous alternatives in most toy and magic shops.

Shooting a Frog into a Globe Light

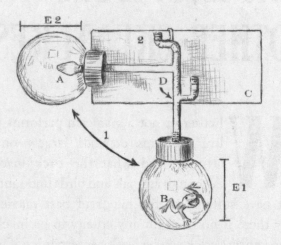

This is a great favourite with children, who like to inspect the live frog before and after the trick. As with so many tricks involving small creatures, it is a moot point as to how much suffering is involved. Probably, incarcerating live frogs in bulbs of glass, and shooting pistol caps alongside their ears is not kind. In former days, magicians were not too hampered by notions of animal rights, and it was once commonplace to perform this particular trick with a bird, which would have been most distressed. I like frogs, and so have devised this trick with plastic models.

The magician explains that in former times, it was customary to do the following trick with canaries which were shot from guns, but he prefers to do the trick with frogs. After this preamble, he produces a frog from thin air, or from a hat. The magician continues, saying that, since the trick is not too kind on frogs, he will put the creature into a temporary trance, before shooting it from a gun. This will guarantee that it feels nothing. It will not even hear the explosion of the gun, while it is in the muzzle. The frog is popped into the stage top hat (on a table), and the magician leans over to make essential hypnotic passes. Then he takes out a very different frog – which is obviously a plastic model. This is usually guaranteed to raise a laugh. He pops the 'entranced' frog into the wide muzzle of a blunderbuss.

On stage, hanging in the space of a simple framework, below some tassel fringing, is a globe containing a light bulb. The magician aims the gun at the globe, and pulls the trigger. There is a loud explosion, the light goes out, and the plastic frog immediately materializes inside the glass bowl. The magician unscrews the globe from its socket, and takes out the frog. Then he drops it into the empty hat, makes a few magic passes, and takes out the original live frog.

HOW THE TRICK IS DONE

There is, in fact, one live frog and two plastic imitations. Before the trick is performed, a plastic frog is placed in the bulb-cover. The second plastic frog is the one originally shown to the audience. The live frog is almost the only real thing in the whole act because the gun and the target are both phoney.

The cap-gun is also phoney, for it has a secret compartment in its blunderbuss barrel. When the plastic frog is dropped into the barrel, it is placed in this secret compartment, to ensure that it cannot be seen after the shot. The light bulb target at which the magician shoots is phoney, though in a far more complicated way.

Unknown to the audience, there are two globes; one contains a shattered light bulb and the second plastic frog and the other contains a lighted bulb. This is the globe which the audience sees at the beginning of the trick, and at which the magician aims the gun. These two globes are arranged on rigid hangers at right angles to each other, in such a way that only one is visible, at any given time, beneath the ornate frame assembly.

At the very moment when the magician fires his blunderbuss at the lighted bulb, an offstage assistant pulls an invisible wire. This releases a catch, which holds the mechanism in place against the pressure of a spring. As a result, the powerful spring pulls down the upper globe, which contains the frog and shattered light bulb, to swap places with the lighted globe, which swings upwards out of sight.

The change takes place so quickly that no one in the audience realizes that it is not the same globe. The impression is that the gun has fired the frog into the globe, as a result of which the light bulb has been broken. Any vibration of lamp-fragments, bowl, frog or ornate fringe (caused by the globes swinging under the pressure of the spring) only adds to the realism of the gun-shot having passed into the lamp, through the bowl. Transforming the plastic frog back into the original live version (which is hidden in a false bottom of the hat for the short duration of the trick) will distract the audience's attention from trying to work out exactly how the magic is worked.

∽∾

The Astrological Spider

On stage is a circular painting of the 12 signs of the zodiac, mounted on a large colourful background. The magician announces to the audience that a modern astrologer has recently proposed that there is a 13th sign of the zodiac. This 13th sign is called Arachne, or 'The Spider'. As he finishes his patter, the magician takes from a box a very large spider. Although the monster is a convincing plastic spider, its appearance will probably be greeted by screams of anguish from sundry members of the audience.

The magician places the creature on the zodiacal circle. Immediately, it scuttles to the sign of Leo. The magician explains that the spider has been trained to do this, because Leo is his own personal sign. This, as he points out, is the sign of the sensitive, gifted and creative showman. But, joking apart, this spider is very clever. In fact, the spider is so clever that it can do astrology and can identify the sun sign of anyone who cares to ask.

Members of the audience are invited to shout out their dates of birth. As soon as they do this, the spider scurries to the relevant segment of the zodiac.

HOW THE TRICK IS DONE

Not surprisingly, the spider is not trained, and knows nothing about the art of astrology. But although this may seem to be a simple trick, it actually involves a considerable stage mechanism. Incidentally, the magician's introductory patter about the 13th sign of the zodiac, Arachne, might sound like nonsense, yet it is quite true.

The astrological spider works because it has a magnet tucked into its belly. Hidden behind the zodiac display is a hardboard circle, its own centre pinned upon the centre of the zodiac, so that it can revolve freely. On this piece of hardboard backing is a powerful magnet, which is

positioned so that it can move around the back of the circle of zodiacal images.

When the magician places the spider on the zodiac, he puts it over the place where he knows the magnet is located. Thus, it is firmly attracted to the vertical surface. When the hidden hardboard circle is moved, the spider is dragged along the circumference of the zodiac. The hardboard circle and magnet are operated by an assistant behind, completely hidden from the view of the audience. If the magician wishes to work the trick using an easel (to show that there really is no trickery), then there needs to be a more complicated arrangement to turn the hidden circle. The mechanism which ensures the right movement, and the right points of arrest, is still operated by an accomplice – this time, offstage. The easiest way to operate this mechanism is to run a string around a central wheel, itself centred on the hardboard circle. In order to give the captive spider the ability to visit each of the 12 zodiacal images, the string must be crossed over, at the bottom. Each of the lengths runs down the back of the easel's legs, and under the curtains behind.

A pull on the left-hand string will turn the spider anticlockwise, while a pull on the right-hand string will turn it in a clockwise direction. To ensure that there is an exact correspondence between the movement of the string and the position of the spider, the ends of the string must be pulled against a suitable calibration. This should mark the corresponding dates of the year and the segments of the 12 signs of the zodiac to which they relate. This calibration must be carefully worked out before starting the show, and the feet of the easel must be placed on a pre-marked spot. It goes without saying that in both versions of the trick the assistant must know which dates fall into which sign of the zodiac for the performance to be successful!

ॐ

Cutting off the Head of a Monster

Magicians who enjoy telling a spellbinding story will revel in this trick. It is a variation on an ancient theme, and tends to go down well with younger audiences, in particular.

At the beginning of the illusion, a large model of a prehistoric monster is revealed onstage. Alternatively, the model is wheeled onto the stage by assistants, its large feet concealing the wheels. The magician explains that the monster is to be executed for having devoured a local princess: indeed so incensed is this dead princess's sister that she plans to carry out the execution herself.

At this point, the magician's assistant, dressed as a princess from the Arabian Nights, steps forward and slices right through the monster's neck with a curved sword. Although the line of the cut is visible, its head does not

THE BOOK OF MAGIC

fall off. Seemingly furious at this failure, she cuts through the neck again – and again – yet still the monster's head holds firm. The princess looks at the creature in amazement and confides to the audience that this must be a truly magic monster. She fears that she should not have dared to attempt the execution and, to make amends, she fills a bucket with a 'magical elixir'. This she offers to the monster, which drinks all the liquid – to the last drop – through its 'severed' throat.

This is perhaps the most remarkable of the magical wonders to have survived from antiquity. As a magic act, it was described by Hero of Alexandria, in an early book on magic, *The Pneumatics*, a collection of 78 tricks, written in the first century AD. In those days, the trick was done with a horse rather than a monster. According to some accounts, the decapitation of a model horse was among the magic tricks performed in front of the Macedonian King of Egypt, Ptolemy Eurgetes, who died in 204 BC.

In this version, the sword really does go through the neck, and the head really does fail to fall off, even though there are no supporting external wires. Moreover, the liquid – which is water in reality – is actually sucked up through the 'severed' neck and so, in a sense, there is no illusion.

HOW THE TRICK IS DONE

The whole operation is made possible by a clever mechanism. Inside the neck of the model are cogged wheels and a gripper plate which permit the sword to cut through the neck without severing it.

The sword blade, in its passage through the monster's neck, strikes a triangular plate with gripper arms on three sides (red in this mechanism). At any given time, one of these grippers must curve around the raised minor segment (which is yellow) on the head-side of the neck, thus holding the two parts of the neck together.

Under pressure from the sword blade, the plate turns on its axis, allowing the blade to slide through. As this happens, the lower gripper disengages, while the top gripper engages the yellow segment on the head-side of the neck. Thus, although the sword passes through the top of the neck, the mechanism still grips the head firmly in place.

When the sword continues downwards, it meets the first of two cogged plates. Once again, the movement of the blade pushes the plate around on its central pivot. In this case, the cogs on the wheel are so arranged as to pull the yellow cogged phalange away from the neck. In turn, this disconnects the water-pipe, leaving the passage clear for the descending blade. Finally, the sword strikes the lower cogged wheel. This has the effect of sliding the yellow cogged phalange back into place, thereby reconnecting the water-pipe. The sword has passed through the neck, spinning the three circular plates in such a way as to complete the illusion. At the end of this process, the mechanism adjusts so that the water-pipe is in place and the creature can 'drink the magical elixir'.

Before the invention of the electric water-pump, the water used to be sucked through the mouth-pipe by means of a partial vacuum in the body, or lower support, of the creature being executed. When the trick is performed today, a water-pump, switched on near the mouth of the monster, is secretly activated by the assistant when she holds up the bucket.

CHAPTER 6

SEANCES, SPIRITUAL ILLUSIONS AND TRANSFORMATIONS

I f you have mastered the majority of the passes, sleights of hand and deceits described so far, you should have learned enough about elementary magic to throw yourself into a variety of different tricks, many of which lie outside the realms of using coins and cards. The following tricks and illusions will amuse your audience and give you a chance to learn a bit more.

A Crystal Ball Trick

The magician's assistant, who he will call 'Madam X', is playing the role of a psychic or clairvoyant, seated in front of a table. On the table is a crystal ball and a tray. In fact, there may also be other objects, such as a rabbit's foot, amulets, talismans, books of magic, and so on. These objects play no part in the trick. In the business, they are called 'glamour tools', or 'glamour ghouls'. They are intended to distract attention, and to mystify.

The magician invites a 'client' from the audience to sit in front of Madam X, on one side of the magical crystal ball. He is asked to write a question on a sheet of paper. He then places this paper, unread by the medium, in an envelope, which he seals, and hands it to the medium.

For a moment or two, Madam X presses the envelope against her forehead, to 'read' it by psychic means. Then, casually, she places it on the tray. She leans over the tray, and looks into the crystal ball, seeking guidance. To the wonderment of the client, she then proceeds to tell him what the question was, and to answer it from signs seen in the crystal.

HOW THE TRICK IS DONE

The table is covered with a thick cloth, tasselled in the best psychic workshop manner. The crystal ball, which could be a less-expensive glass ball, rests on the table cover. Alongside is the tray, the peculiar nature of which accounts for how the deceit works. What the client cannot see is that the bottom of the tray is transparent. Nor is he aware that the oblong of cloth below the tray is cut away and that the top of the table is made of glass.

Beneath the glass table-top, yet hidden by the cover of cloth, is a shaded light which illuminates the underside of the table-top. When this light is switched on, the bottom of the tray is discreetly lit.

As Madam X leans over the tray (which is now partly hidden from the view of the client) she presses a foot-switch to light up the tray. The light is sufficiently bright and localized for her to read the message through the envelope.

If the medium finds that the message is the wrong way round, she can always pick it up, and press it against her forehead again, to improve the 'vibrations'. When she puts it down, she is careful to ensure that it is replaced on the correct side for reading. How Madam X succeeds in answering the question, which, of course, may relate to some future event, is the real mystery and requires humorous invention! In any event, the audience will be impressed that she has read the question.

∾

The Spirit Table

The magician, who may be a fraudulent medium, or one playing the role of a fraudulent medium, invites a group of people to sit around a small table. They have been invited to a demonstration of a seance, 'to make contact with the other world'. The room is suitably darkened. There may be a vase of flowers on the table, because it is well-known that spirits like the smell of flowers. There may also be discreet music, for the same reason. The whole scene is contrived to create the mysterious atmosphere of a seance.

Everyone sits around the table, in semi-darkness, with their hands palm-side down and fingers just touching. The magician, in a deliberate, sonorous voice, asks, 'Is anybody there?' At the third asking, the table gives a little shudder. After a moment or so, much to the surprise of those present, the table begins to float upwards into the air, where it rocks gently for some time.

Houdini, who was the terror of the fraudulent medium, saw the dramatic potential in these spirit-cons, and performed them on a darkened stage. He once caught out a fraudulent psychic by placing shoe blacking on the end of a trumpet, prior to a seance. During the seance, the trumpet was mysteriously sounded by spirit agencies, and after the seance, there was much cynical laughter when it was discovered that the medium's lips were black.

HOW THE TRICK IS DONE

The darkness of the seance room aids this sort of trickery. Specialists say that there are over ten ways of lifting tables, not one of which involves invisible spirits. Here are two ways that a table can be fraudulently made to fly.

The medium hides a knife up the sleeve of her coat or jacket. In the darkness, she slides the tip of the knife under the table edge, places her hands flat on the table, and participates as innocently as the others, 'waiting for the spirits to move and lift the table'. When the table moves, it is of course the medium raising it by lifting her arm and the secret knife.

An alternative method requires a little more preparation in advance. Before the seance, the medium has driven a small nail into the table-top, in front of the place where she habitually sits. She then slips a ring on her finger beneath the head of the nail, and lifts the table undetected.

This levitating table may be combined with the hocus-pocus of the next trick, which offers a diet of Mysterious Raps from the Other Side. In fact, a whole mock seance can be worked into a sophisticated entertainment, in which levitating tables, spirit-raps and ghostly visitations culminate in a convincing materialization of a spirit. Such a performance would be entirely in accord with the seance-entertainments which flourished in Victorian times, and which were popular well into the 1950s, as many magicians' posters testify.

Tricks with a levitating table depend mainly upon the darkness of the seance room. The reason why some fraudulent mediums like to have a vase of flowers on the table has nothing to do with the olfactory sensitivities of spirits. When the flowers begin to slide off the table, at the beginning of the performance, it adds a sense of drama to the event. More important, however, it establishes for those in the darkness, who are to some extent suffering from sense deprivation, that the table really is moving about.

Many photographs, usually taken by crude flash techniques, have survived of mediums demonstrating table-lifting in seances. These darkroom seances were especially popular in Victorian times, but some of the finest photographs were taken in the 1920s: it goes without saying that most of these were of fraudulent activities.

ఌఞ

Mysterious Raps from the Other Side

This is an extension of the seance described above. A group of people are invited to sit around a table in order to make contact with the spirit world. In the darkness, sounds and raps are made, none of which appear to come from the 'medium' or magician who is conducting the seance. This phenomenon, nearly always practised in a dimly lit seance room, depends for its effectiveness on the fact that it is very difficult for people to tell from which direction a sound is actually coming, when they are in darkness. If a medium says that a particular sound is coming from a table – or, for that matter, from any object – then that is where the participants will imagine the sound is coming from.

HOW THE TRICK IS DONE

Medium-baiters claim that there are more than 25 ways of producing spirit raps, in ways which will easily evade detection. This, however, is how the most popular 'rapping' fraud works.

The medium wears a specially prepared shoe. One of the heels is hollow and has inside a small hammer arrangement. The head of the hammer is held back by a rubber band and tied to a piece of cotton or fine string, which runs up to the top of medium's leg. If those present are not holding hands, the medium can pull the cotton so that the hammer strikes home, and makes a convincing rapping noise. In most seances, however, the medium's hands will be held by others to ensure that there is no trickery. In this instance, the cotton is tied to a garter at the top of her leg. When she flexes her knee, the spirits will rap!

The possible arrangement for the spring-hammer and cotton are almost endless. Some mediums have a complicated, yet well-hidden, system of strings running under the floor-boards, operated by a foot pedal. Others even have two or three such strings, sometimes running up to hammers set in the legs of their seance tables.

Mediums have always claimed that rapping is one of the methods used by spirits trapped on the 'other side'. It is their way of making contact with the living. In seances, when rapping is heard, questions may be asked of the spirits. It is agreed that one rap means 'Yes', and two raps mean 'No'. This is certainly an important stock in trade of fraudulent mediums who wish to impress, and probably fleece, their clients.

❦

Madam Nordica's Magic Chair

The magician takes the audience into his confidence, and tells them that, when he was a child, his ambition was to be a medium. To achieve this, he studied under the famous clairvoyant, Madam Nordica, from whom he learned a number of tricks which are useful in creating poltergeists', and other spiritist 'manifestations'. He smiles at the audience, and insists that he will try to do better than the fraud, Harry Price, who photographed a brick as it was falling, and then claimed that the brick had been thrown by one of the Borley Rectory poltergeists. After all, if you see a brick being thrown through the air, is it likely that you will have time to whip out your camera and take its photograph?

Following this initial patter, the magician explains that Madam Nordica taught him how to mesmerize chairs and tables, which he will now demonstrate. He makes a few passes at a chair, which begins to jerk about, as though shuffling on its feet. He then turns his attention to a table, and works similar magic upon this. It also starts to move about.

Music strikes up, and the table and chair begin to dance in time, becoming more and more hectic as the tempo increases. There is really no end to the number of objects which can be made to move in this way. Manipulation is the name of the game when the spiritualist sets out to astonish or entertain.

HOW THE TRICK IS DONE

There are two simple ways to make tables or chairs dance to your command. In the first, both chair and table are moved by an assistant offstage. They are wired separately, but in such a way that they will tilt, and while balancing precariously on one or two of their legs, may be dragged along. This takes at least three wires for each object.

The assistant, by pulling first on one wire, and then on another, can make the table or chair involve itself in all sorts of gyrations. However, brilliant showmanship by the magician makes the performance believable, for the audience has the distinct impression that it is his own magnetized hands which make the objects dance as if by magic.

To be effective, the trick is best performed against a dark background, which helps to obscure the wires from the audience. It is also a good idea to have the objects painted in a light colour, such as silver, though when this is done, it is important to make sure that the wires are tied around parts of the object (such as finials or moulding joints) where they will not be visible.

An easier way to perform the trick is for the magician to have a single string running from his waistcoat to the back of the chair. As he moves backwards, as though mesmerizing it, the chair will rear up on its far legs, and begin to edge towards him. Although this trick may sound a little far-fetched, if you try it for yourself, you will see just how effective it is.

༄༅

The Ghost of Uncle Fred

While he is on the subject of Madam Nordica (his first teacher), the magician tells his audience that, under her tuition, he learned how to produce ectoplasm at will and how to mould the ectoplasm into human form. Indeed, he is so adroit with ectoplasm, that, under the right conditions, he can invite Uncle Fred to come back from the dead.

Nowadays, the magician explains, we do not call such phenomena 'ghosts' – they are 'materializations', and these can only take place under proper seance conditions. This means there must be almost total darkness because spirits do not like the light. To create the right atmosphere, the magician might also add that tampering with the spiritual world can be dangerous, so now would be a good time for any faint-hearted members of the audience to leave.

A cabinet is wheeled onstage, and is shown to be empty. The magician puts his assistant into a trance, and she enters the cabinet, zombie-like. The lights dim – not quite to total darkness, but sufficiently for the illusion to take place. Slowly, a mass of 'ectoplasm' emerges from the cabinet, and begins to move towards the audience. At first, it is quite small, and of an indeterminate shape. Gradually, however, it takes form, rears up, and takes shape.

After a few dramatic ghostly gestures, and perhaps a little moaning, Uncle Fred's phantasm sinks back to earth. Soon, it is only a couple of feet high – a formless ectoplasm once more. This floats almost to the ranks of the audience, but then begins to grow smaller, returning to its former state. Finally, it disappears completely. The lights are switched on, to reveal an exhausted assistant, still in a trance. The magician snaps his fingers, and calls her back to the realms of the living.

If there is time enough, this illusion offers ample opportunity for all sorts of dramatic or humorous enterprise. If he is so inclined, the magician can take messages from the dead, and the potential for fun is endless. The audience knows that the magician is putting on a purely entertaining show, and will not take it seriously, as unfortunately happens in certain seance gatherings, even today.

HOW THE TRICK IS DONE

As mediums themselves know, there are many ways of materializing varieties of 'Uncle Fred' or whoever. As with similar seance tricks, the whole effect of this particular ghostly entertainment depends upon the relative darkness of the stage. Just as 'spirits' do not like the light, nor do mediums.

As you might suspect, the assistant is not in a trance and, she is very much aware of her role in the trick. In among her clothing, she has concealed a telescopic tube. At the end of this is a balloon, around which tatters of white silk or cheesecloth have been stuck. Alternatives to the balloon are a telescopic wire funnel, or a cage. These are the potential ectoplasm.

In performances where it is not possible to hide this essential equipment, fraudulent mediums tend to resort to using a small trolley. This is little more than a short plank, mounted on wheels, which may be pulled by means of an invisible wire from the back of the room – where it is hidden out of sight under the drapes of a screen. The load upon this trolley is extremely small, but will expand incredibly to achieve the desired effect.

Having entered the cabinet, the assistant obtains the load, in one way or another, and then pushes the loaded telescopic tube outwards, through a hole in the curtain. As she does so, she blows gently into it, to inflate the balloon. If a wire cage is being used, she releases the string which holds the wire cage on the end of the tubing, to allow 'Uncle Fred' to drop to his full height. In the darkness, the balloon, or cage, makes a strange metamorphosis.

At this point the ghost-like materialization does not look like Uncle Fred, but it will scare anyone not familiar with the trick. It may look almost benign in full light, yet when seen in the semi-light of a darkened seance room, it appears ghoulish and frightening. The balloon must be as full as possible, and then lifted (by the blow-tube) off the ground, to allow the filaments of silk to drop down. Alternatively, the compressed cage must be released, to drop vertically and hang from the tube. These actions permit the second phase of the operation to take place.

The second stage of the trick requires that, once the 'ectoplasm' has reached its largest extent, it is used as a shield, to obscure the fact that an assistant, her face liberally daubed with white make-up, and her body draped in voluminous white sheets, is crawling under the curtains. The assistant and the ectoplasm merge only for a moment. Slowly, the assistant rises, to simulate the materialization of Uncle Fred. The darkness is on her side, but she should not stay fully materialized as Uncle Fred for too long. Almost as quickly as the shape arrives, it should disappear, using the ectoplasm as a shield to hide the escape route through the curtains.

You might think that these 'manifestations' sound too crude to fool anyone – but they have taken in many past audiences. A number of photographs of 'materialized spirits' are genuine records of materializations perpetrated in Victorian seances which were sufficiently convincing to fool psychic investigators and scientists.

CXO

Seeing with X-ray Eyes

Originally a parlour trick in Victorian times, versions of this trick were taken over by fraudulent mediums, who sought to demonstrate what would today be called Extra Sensory Perception. Few accounts of the investigation into mediumistic fraud are as amusing and well-observed as that which Houdini did on the fraudulent Argamasilla, 'The Spaniard with X-ray Eyes'. This man, who claimed to be able to see through metal, was revealed to be only a conjurer who was able to fool many 'psychic investigators', until he came up against Houdini.

Such frauds gave this trick a bad name, but versions of it are now returning as a standard piece of magicology among those who perform for small audiences. The trick demands a fairly intimate audience, and is rarely successful in a large hall, because of the size of the equipment involved. It is also very easy to perform, so this is a good opportunity for the magician's assistant to take over for a while and show that she, too, has magical skills.

The assistant presents to the audience three decorated boxes, about 23 cm x 13 cm (9 in x 5 in), and about 5 cm (2 in) deep. Into each of these boxes are fitted small blocks of equal size. One of these three blocks is decorated with a clown, and a member of the audience is invited to examine all the boxes.

THE BOOK OF MAGIC

The assistant explains that she is fortunate to have the gift of X-ray vision, which she augments with the aid of a magnifying glass. She shows the glass, and even hands it round for examination, explaining that, for those without the gift of X-ray vision, it works only as an ordinary magnifier.

A member of the audience is asked to place each of the three blocks in the three boxes. While this is being done, the assistant stands out of the line of vision, possibly with a blindfold over her eyes. Only the audience knows in which box the clown has been placed.

Once the box lids have been closed, the magician takes her magnifying glass, and carefully examines the top of each box. In this way, according to her own account, her developed X-ray vision permits her to see through the wood. After only a short scrutiny, she succeeds in correctly identifying the position of the clown. She does this several times, on each occasion with a different member of the audience choosing the box in which the clown is placed.

HOW THE TRICK IS DONE

The block of wood decorated with the clown has a small magnet inside it. The insertion is clever, because it cannot be seen even when it is inspected closely. The magnet may either be set flush with the wood surface, and covered with a pasted image of a clown. Alternatively, the surface may be painted, in which case the magnet will be covered by the undercoat.

The assistant does not even need to look through the magnifying glass, for the handle reveals all – it has a small magnet hidden inside it. As she appears to be looking through the glass, the assistant is actually dragging the handle over the surface of the boxes, feeling for the delicate 'pull' of the handle which betrays the position of the larger magnet on the clown block inside the box.

Some magicians do not use a magnifying glass. Their gizmo is a small tube, which also 'augments their X-ray vision'. During the arrangement of the boxes, when all attention is on this, the magician palms a compass. This is especially designed so that it slots neatly into the bottom of the X-ray gizmo. When the magician appears to be looking through the magical gizmo, into the box, he is actually looking at the compass dial. By its reaction, he can determine where the magnetized clown is placed in the boxes. Needless to say, the second version of the trick is more difficult to perform because the compass has to be palmed and inserted into the tube.

�❧

The Magical Azoth

This is another trick which is just as effectively performed by the assistant as the magician. At the beginning of the trick, she is holding a long, hollow

THE DAVENPORT BROTHERS'
PUBLIC CABINET SÉANCE.

NOW BEING HELD AT
THE QUEEN'S CONCERT ROOMS,
HANOVER SQUARE.

brass rod. To prove that there is nothing mysterious about it, she hands it to the audience for examination. Once everyone is satisfied, she places it vertically in a weighty holder, or into a special fixture, on the stage floor.

Next, she picks up a large wooden ball which is sprayed gold and has a hole through its centre. Again, she hands the ball to the audience for examination. When it has been scrutinized, she slides it over the top of the rod. It slips gently down to the bottom, and rests on the support. Some magicians like to perform this trick with a human skull instead of a ball but an audience is not usually as keen to handle this.

The assistant 'magnetizes' her hands by washing them in a special blue liquid which she has concocted. This liquid, she tells the audience, is the ancient alchemical Azoth, recently rediscovered in modern times. She demonstrates that she does not need to dry her hands, as the liquid itself is already magnetized, and will repel the water. It does not have normal wetting properties.

The assistant makes a few magical passes, and begins to radiate power from her fingers towards the ball, issuing verbal commands. Slowly at first, the ball begins to rise upwards. Then it moves more quickly. As it reaches the top, the assistant orders it to move down again. In fact, the ball will move in any vertical direction, and at any speed, following the command of her hands.

Before the wonder of the trick wears thin, the assistant removes the ball and rod, handing both back to the audience for further scrutiny. This time, however, she warns them to be careful, as the magnetism from the Azoth is catching, and does not fade for over 24 hours.

HOW THE TRICK IS DONE

As you might imagine, the wet-less Azoth has nothing to do with this intriguing piece of magic. Inside the wooden ball is a hollow iron core. The hollow brass tube is slotted into a heavy base. Unknown to the audience, this base has been so placed as to be directly over a hole bored through the stage floor. When the assistant places the ball over the brass tube, and begins the hocus-pocus to levitate it, an unseen accomplice beneath the stage pushes a rod – which has a powerful magnet at the top – up the tube.

When the ball is dropped to the bottom of the brass tube, the assistant makes contact between the magnet and the iron core of the ball. Once contact has been made, the ball can be made to rise and fall at any desired speed, according to the whim of the assistant. The pattern of such movements either needs to be well rehearsed in advance, or the accomplice must listen closely to the assistant's patter, and act accordingly.

The magical Azoth liquid is only coloured water. Before the performance, the assistant rubs Lycopodium powder on her hands, or floats it on the surface of the water. This enables her to place her hands in the water without wetting them.

൭൪

Cagliostro's Skull

In magicological terms, this trick is genuine 'black magic'. The magician places a skull in a glass cabinet and closes the glass front. He tells the audience that this is the skull of the noted occultist, Cagliostro, and that even in death, the famous Italian still exhibits magical powers. Amazingly, his skull can answer questions: it will rise once to indicate 'Yes,' twice to indicate 'No', and if it does not know the answer, it will spin around.

The only proviso, the magician warns, is that Cagliostro's skull cannot answer questions about the future. Legend has it that if such a question is asked, then the skull will fragment for ever. The magician therefore begs the audience to be most careful about the questions posed, because he does not want the skull, which has such a famed antiquity, to be destroyed.

At the beginning, the magician himself asks some simple questions, and the skull answers accordingly, rising and falling in a most extraordinary way. Having demonstrated the magical power of the skull, the magician opens up the questioning to the audience. All goes well until the time arrives (as is bound to happen!) when someone in the audience asks a question about the future.

The skull spins round rapidly and then begins to rise higher and higher. There is a puff of smoke from within the cabinet, and the skull completely disappears.

This macabre piece of hocus-pocus is an especial delight for children. Rising skulls, in one form or another, have been a standard stage property for hundreds of years, and a few mechanical versions have survived from Victorian theatre. One of the magical sketches worked out by Maskelyne and Cooke for their performances in the Egyptian Hall, Piccadilly, involved an entire skeleton. Illuminated on stage, it did a jig, and eventually the rattling jaw and skull divorced from the rest of the body, and floated into the auditorium, over the heads of a scared audience. This piece of magic, all done by wires, seems to have been performed in a dimly lit hall, and the new-fangled gas-lights were specially lowered for the effect. For all its ancient origins, however, the popularity of the skull seems never to wane.

HOW THE TRICK IS DONE

When the magician places the skull in the glass cabinet, he ensures that it is resting on a black rod. This rod cannot be seen by the audience, against the black background of the stage set. The black rod slides securely through the central leg-support of the glass case, and is long enough to obtrude through the stage floor. The rod is worked from this hidden vantage point. When the magician wishes the skull to rise, an assistant below-stage pushes the glass rod upwards. When the skull is required to fall, the assistant allows it to slip down. To make the skull spin, the assistant simply spins the rod between his or her hands.

The curtain behind the glass cage must be black. This colour helps to add a touch of the macabre to the act, but it also serves a most useful purpose. Above the glass case, though set back a little from its outer edges, is a second black curtain, which cannot be distinguished from the one behind it. When the time comes for the skull to vanish, the assistant pushes the rod upwards to its extreme extension. The skull is thereby hidden behind the small black curtain, and appears to have vanished. If real sophistication is required, then the magician can install a simple gripping device behind the curtain, which takes hold of the skull. While the smoke is still hanging in the air, the curtain and skull can be rapidly raised, and the glass rod is allowed to drop into the cage support, out of sight. When the smoke clears, the skull really has disappeared.

A further sophistication is that a bag of broken shards ('the exploded skull') can be opened from behind the curtain at the very moment that the skull vanishes. Instead of seeming to vanish, the skull then appears to have exploded.

For details on how to produce smoke onstage, see the Glossary, on page 231.

∾

The Bronze Head of Michael Scot

The magician tells the story of Michael Scot, a 13th-century monk who invented a talking head, made from bronze. When this wizard died, he was buried in Melrose Abbey in Scotland, where his tomb may be seen to this day. It was rumoured that the bronze automaton had been buried with him. However, when the grave was dug up in the last century, the casket inside the coffin was said to have been empty. Some locals insist that grave-robbers stole the head, and that it was sold into a disreputable school of black magicians.

As he talks, the magician pulls aside a curtain to reveal a box, on a small table. The magician lifts up the box up to reveal a mechanical – though extremely life-like – bronze head. Its eyes are closed, as though it is asleep. The audience can see that the head is totally disembodied, because underneath it there is only the undraped table, through which the curtains behind are visible.

The magician continues, 'Is this remarkable head the original bronze automaton of Michael Scot? Perhaps it is, for it has the power to talk, and can answer questions of profound import.' So saying, the magician raps the table with his magic wand and the automaton opens its eyes and speaks. The magician begins to ask it questions, and each time the head responds accurately.

Members of the audience are then invited to ask questions, to which the head replies. After a while, the head explains that the heat of the stage lighting is drying up its powers. It longs for the cold of his master's tomb, and must leave. Although the magician tries to stop it, there is a slight puff of smoke, and the head disappears, leaving the table empty.

There are several variants of this trick, which some claim was learned by European conjurers from Indian fakirs. In fact, the talking automaton was a popular adjunct of many ancient occultists. Even earlier than Scot, the extraordinary magician, Gerbert, an 11th-century astrologer, had the same useful toy to help him. He was described as one who had so much power that 'the demons obeyed in all that he required of them day and night, because of ... his magic books and a great diversity of rings and candles.' Although a much-feared magician, if only by reputation, Gerbert eventually became Pope. Even after his elevation, he was reputed to have had a spirit which lived in a golden head, which would answer questions put to it. It is reported that Gerbert and this magical golden head together composed an important commentary on arithmetic. This connection with Gerbert, and with Michael Scot, who was a follower of this master in astrological lore if not in conjuration, suggests that the trick came from a Middle Eastern source, since both were great

Arabic scholars. Perhaps the Arabic documents in which they discovered the secret was a translation of a work by Hero of Alexandria, who bequeathed so many of the magical devices of the ancient world in his book *The Automatic Theatre*.

Those who have watched this astonishing trick tend to believe that it relies on clever ventriloquism. However, this would not explain how the head's mouth and eyes move so convincingly. In fact, there is no need for such a specialist practice as voice-throwing, because the head does really talk and answer the questions put to it.

The origins of this version of the trick can be traced not to Delhi or Alexandria, but to London. It was one of the more notable inventions of T.W. Tobin, who worked at the Royal Polytechnic Institute in Regent Street, along with the more famous magician, 'Professor' Pepper.

HOW THE TRICK IS DONE

Like many other illusions, the trick is done with mirrors. First, the head is that of a living woman, who sits behind the table. But the mystery lies more in the table than in the woman.

The table, set in a curtained alcove, is a three-legged round design, with one of the legs directed towards the audience. Two mirrors have been cleverly framed by the table legs on either side: these mirrors meet invisibly, framed by the central leg. This mirror-framing means that, on each side, the half-leg of the table is reflected into a whole leg, and the side curtains are reflected in the space between. From the audience's viewpoint, the table looks solid and as if it has curtains draped behind it.

Only the head of the woman is visible. In reality, she is sitting comfortably on a chair, her body hidden by the mirrors. If you decide to mount this illusion, you must take into account the nature of the floor upon which the table stands. If you are not careful, the angle of reflection of the surface may reveal the presence of the mirrors. The flooring must be a flat, even colour, or perhaps with a square pattern, but it must be a design that will not give the game away.

Since the talking head is a real woman, who is not at all uncomfortable in this decapitated condition, she is genuinely able to answer the questions put to her. Strong and distinctive make-up – especially a liberal application of gold stage-paint – ensures that the head has a mechanical or otherwise inhuman look to it.

❦

Metempsychosis

The magician explains to the audience that reincarnation has nothing to do with passing from lifetime to lifetime, as occultists claim. If you are dissatisfied with your present life, then you can change it. All you need is the secret spell. Many years ago, the magician continues, he had the good fortune (and sufficient backsheesh), to learn this secret spell from an Egyptian magician who he met in the corridors of the Great Pyramid. As a result, he now has a considerable clientele of wealthy elderly people seeking instant reincarnation – usually in the bodies of attractive and wealthy young people!

However, before demonstrating this art, the magician confides that there is a degree of danger in this tampering with nature. Something in the Egyptian magic was not perfect – perhaps the Gnostic mantra was not pronounced properly. Occasionally – but fortunately, rarely – the process goes wrong.

As he speaks, an old witch hobbles on stage. She has with her a cat. Altogether, she looks like a most suitable candidate for transformation. With a few passes from the magician (and some show of reciting a Gnostic mantra), she gradually fades away. Her form is replaced by a very shadowy figure of a young girl, which gradually becomes clearer and clearer, until she is revealed as a youthful beauty. The magician is satisfied. However, the cat, which so far has been sitting obediently at his side, runs towards the young beauty. As the cat disappears, a monstrous bear begins to form, and runs onstage.

The magic has gone wrong. The magician panics and all riot is let loose. The beauty is so surprised that she backs away, and is transformed into a vampire. The magician tries to escape her embrace, and, in turn, is transformed into a huge gorilla. A mayhem of transformations proceeds, much to the hilarity of the audience. At last, the magician is reincarnated into his original form, and puts an end to the show with a few magic spells.

This remarkable series of illusions is usually said to have been the invention of 'Professor' Pepper. When this great Victorian magician is remembered at all, it is usually for his famous stage ghost, raised not by black magic means, but with the aid of glass. However, Pepper was a clever inventor of several 'scientific' devices which permitted most original and sensational performances of magic. It is likely that this illusion was the one used in the ancient temples, to awe or scare worshippers. It is among some of the illusions recorded by the 1st-century magician, Hero of Alexandria. In that time, devices were used to supply temples and altars with statues, or automata, of a miraculous nature. It is possible that the famous bull, which floated in the air inside the temple of Serapis, in Egypt, was one of these reflection illusions.

With the aid of such magic, priests could arrange for giant statues to move and talk, for ghosts to appear and disappear, and for magicians to throw objects into the air, where they would disappear. I like to think that the mechanisms discovered in the ancient Necromanteion at Ephyra, in Greece, were linked with the use of mirrors. In the dim light of this underground cell, priests were reputed to 'bring back the dead spirits'. Dating from 1000 BC, it must be the oldest surviving stage mechanism in the world. Of course, it is possible that the ancient priests who served this oracle really did know how to invoke genuine spirits, but it is more likely that they were practising stage magic. This suggestion is quite reasonable. For example, Hero of Alexandria left instructions on how to arrange things so that a supplicant approaching an altar might suddenly be confronted by the sight of a god slowly materializing from nowhere. He even devised a trick whereby two mirrors were arranged to open and close on a common axis, allowing the goddess Pallas Athena, in her armour, to spring from the head of Zeus, as one version of the Greek myths insists did happen.

When it came to actual performances, the Victorian 'Professor' Pepper was much more of a humorist than Hero, and yet just as dramatic as ancient Greek priests. In his own version of Transmigration, Pepper would offer to change a bowl of sausages back into 'the animal from which they were made'. Inevitably, as the sausages faded away, the audience expected it to turn into a healthy pig. Instead, they transformed into a delightful white poodle!

It has been suggested that Lewis Carroll (who was an amateur conjurer, and a keen fan of magical performances) almost certainly took his idea of the disappearing Cheshire Cat in *Alice in Wonderland* from Pepper's ghost illusions. As Alice points out, it is one thing to see a cat without a smile, but quite a different thing to see a smile without a cat. This latter could be achieved with Pepper's mirrors.

HOW THE TRICK IS DONE

This particular illusion is another Pepper trick, all done with mirrors. The preparation for the full illusion is truly awesome, but it is satisfying to perform because it never fails to amaze. A most convincing equivalent of the full-size trick may be worked in miniature, with the aid of puppets, toys and marionettes.

The secret of this trick lies in the preparation, and positioning onstage, of a huge mirror, at an angle to the stage. Half is an ordinary mirror, the other half is pure glass. A considerable vertical area between the two is graduated silver backing, fading from pure silvering to pure glass. In Pepper's day, this half-silvering was laboriously obtained by scraping away the backing. Today, it is possible to remove the silver on the mirror by sanding it carefully with wire-wool. Most proficient glaziers will be able to provide a half-silvered mirror, which may be treated in this way.

The mirror used in this series of puppet transformations is about 1.8 m (6 ft) wide and 1.2 m (4 ft) high. The whole mirror-glass is set at an angle across the stage, so that the mirror reflects the curtains, to give an impression of continuity. Lighting is just as important as the angle of the glass, so a good deal of experimentation is required to make the illusion work convincingly.

Anyone standing behind the front curtain will be seen reflected in the glass. All that is required to perform the illusion is for one person to move using the same gestures and speed behind the glass, in continuance of the movement of the reflected figure. The principle offers endless opportunities for dramatic invention, but the technique is most suited to humour. It is largely impractical for the amateur to prepare, house and display a sheet of glass of sufficient size to work the illusion with people on a stage. However, it is relatively simple to prepare the illusion on a smaller scale, perhaps using a toy theatre with articulated models such as marionettes and swinging toys, which will be particularly popular in a children's entertainment. An interesting challenge for an amateur would be to construct the illusion so as to metamorphose the smiling face of a cat into an isolated feline smile.

CHAPTER 7

❖━━━❖❖❖━━━❖

SEEING IS BELIEVING

The following illusions are more complicated for an amateur to perform, but it is still fascinating to know some of the techniques involved. Although audiences usually like to guess how a trick is done, the magician can do much to divert the attention of onlookers who may be on the right track. The fact is that even if people suspect that an illusion is performed with mechanical aids and magic equipment, they must respond according to what they can see with their own eyes.

The Art of Levitation

Levitation is probably the most popular of all magical illusions, and most reputable performers have one version or another to offer onstage. Among the most remarkable of the Victorian performances (when levitation was an essential attribute of every performer) was that done by the great Maskelyne in the Egyptian Hall, in 1876. This was indeed a 'Levitation Extraordinary', as the newspapers put it, for instead of there being a secret mechanism, partly hidden by curtains and poor illumination, the whole stage was brightly lit. The progress of the floating magician was followed by powerful beams of light, as he inched his way like an air-fish, first over the proscenium, and then into the auditorium, where he floated over the heads of the astonished audience. Rising higher, he levitated into the cupola

over the centre of the room. After hovering there for a few minutes, he floated back to the stage, where he landed horizontally, in the same position as he had begun

For all its difficulties, aerial suspension was a favourite trick of Robert-Houdin, probably the greatest of Victorian magicians. Although he was not the first to present the floating woman act, he was the first to stage it as though the levitation was induced by chemical means – the woman floated after she had been persuaded to drink a liquid 'ether'. Of course, Houdin was merely keeping his magician's finger on the pulse of the times; the wonders of scientific discoveries had still not lost their freshness for the Victorians. (It may seem surprising today but the inventors of the first electric lamp, Robert-Houdin's contemporaries, stared at it in rapt wonder, without eating or sleeping, for over 48 hours. And when one magician suggested that future cities might be lit by electric lamps, he was booed by the audience which thought the idea inconceivable.)

If electricity was not fully appreciated, the less-scientific 'ether' was. Robert-Houdin called his act, 'Suspension Ethereene', and practised it in public on his young son (shown in mid-air on the previous page). The child drank the magical liquid, and was then balanced on poles. All but one were removed, to leave him suspended. Some members of the audience, considering this child abuse, were outraged, and the magician had many problems with the act.

Times have changed and audiences know that no ill treatment is involved in modern magic. Whatever the chicanery, drama or humour built around the act, the illusion itself is much the same, the world over.

❧

The Floating Woman

In a modern version of the art of 'levitation', the magician's assistant is mesmerized by her master. She begins to lean backwards, until the angle she is at is theoretically impossible. After a few magic passes, her feet begin to leave the ground, and she begins to turn, on a lateral axis, with a fulcrum somewhere near the small of her back. In other words, she begins to levitate. Soon she is floating in a horizontal position. The magician then passes a hoop over the length of her body, to prove that she is not suspended by any material structure.

HOW THE TRICK IS DONE

There are two parts to this floating lady illusion. First, the assistant begins to lean over backwards. This is made possible by a strong metal rod, which has been pushed up through a hole in the stage. As she leans backwards, the assistant is supported by the rod, and is manipulated to the required angle.

The second part of the illusion takes over when, according to all the laws of physics, the assistant should fall over backwards. At this moment, a special mechanism, from back stage, comes into operation. This puts out an arm, at the end of which is a short but comfortable bed. The angle of this bed is such that the assistant can lean against it, at the moment when the rod is withdrawn from the stage floor.

Now the bed begins to twist on its central axis, taking the assistant with it. The impression is that her feet are beginning to float upwards. Eventually, bed and assistant are both horizontal. The hoop with which the magician proves that her body is not supported has a secret join in it, so that it can pass over the supporting mechanism.

ༀ

The Bodiless Lady

In Victorian times, a variation of the rotating woman illusion was performed under the title of 'The Bodiless Lady'. A famous version of this act was 'Zarma', which has survived in a striking wood engraving. This illusion was presented in many different guises.

For example, the magician might stand, dressed as a medieval wizard, alongside a cabinet in which float the head and bust of his assistant, who is dressed as a medieval princess. This half-woman is resting on a table. The magician explains to the audience that she has been bewitched by a black magician, from Castle Bran, for refusing to be eaten by a dragon. The magician is worried because he does not know the right magic spell to release her. The princess then talks to him (to show the audience that she is alive), and her pet dog runs beneath her floating body (to indicate that this is not just a mirror trick). The magician appears to be worried, especially when the girl complains that she is tired of being only half a woman. She becomes petulant – a good magician would surely know what to do! In desperation, the magician looks around. He sees a curtain and a pistol. He drapes the curtain over the girl, and shoots the pistol. The curtain falls, to reveal the princess restored to her entirety.

In this illusion, the lady's upper parts are resting on a table. According to one surviving account of this act, the magician can prove that there is no body below by thrusting a sword through the spaces beneath the table. He can also stab it between the body and the table-top.

HOW THE TRICK IS DONE

At one time, this act was infamous among magician's assistants as being among the most uncomfortable on record. The girl lies on a hammock, slung from the top of the cabinet, or from the flies above the stage. Her head and shoulders are resting on a false body. Because the extended form might be visible from parts of the auditorium, lights are sometimes used to obscure the view.

When the curtain is draped, the false body is attached to the back of this fabric, the hammock is released, and the girl slides down to the floor. She holds the table in her hands. Any support from the hammock is hidden behind the table, pushed into the false top, and so she is free to put the table down.

ઝ૭

The Mismatched Lady

Onstage, or wheeled onstage, is an upright tier of boxes, visibly divided into three or four segments. The whole set is high enough to take a human form, standing upright. Each of the sides, fronts and backs of the four boxes can be opened, as the magician duly demonstrates. The boxes may also stand on a low platform, revealing a space below them: this shows the audience that 'no stage trap door is being used'. (They will obviously not be raised on a platform if a trap door is in fact to be used.)

The magician's assistant, wearing very distinctive and colourful clothes, climbs into the cabinet. The magician opens each of the doors in turn to reveal the three or four different levels of the woman, and to prove that there is no trickery. The magician may chain her in place, developing a line of patter as he does so. Perhaps she has to be chained in this way to ensure that she does not disappear. Once the assistant is inside, the magician hypnotizes her. She falls into a trance – her head sinks to one side, and she is perfectly still.

The magician swings the set of boxes around on a central vertical axis to show that there is nothing untoward at the back. In some box designs, the magician can open up the doors, on all four sides. The assistant is entirely visible, and still in a deep trance.

The magician closes all the doors on the contraption. As he does so, he explains that this is the first time that he has attempted this difficult illusion. He hopes that he is going to perform it well, for otherwise there is a certain danger for the girl inside. Notwithstanding this danger, he pronounces the magic words, and makes the requisite magical passes.

Now the magician opens the top door. The assistant's head has gone. The magician peers into the box from behind. So far the trick is going according to plan. He closes the top door and opens the second door down. This time her upper part has vanished. Once again, the magician peers in from behind, or from the side, and then closes this second door. Continuing the trick, he opens the third door to reveal that her trunk has disappeared. Again, the magician peers in from behind, or from the side, and shuts the door.

The magician is visibly relieved. To make sure that the trick has worked completely, he opens the bottom door but – horror of horrors – here is his assistant's head! Looking very worried, he closes the bottom door and feels around underneath the supporting table. His assistant is not there. Once again, he opens the bottom door but now there is no sign of her.

Relieved, and implying that the trick is over, the magician takes a bow. Then, almost as an afterthought, he checks the top box. When it is open, his assistant's legs can be seen. The trick has gone wrong. Horrified, he quickly opens and closes the different levels, always finding a mismatched lady, or an isolated segment of her body.

Before the novelty wears off, he opens all the doors in turn to discover – with evident relief – that his assistant is whole again with all the parts of her body in the right place. She walks out smiling and unharmed.

HOW THE TRICK IS DONE

Even when you know how this illusion is achieved it is always a delight to see it performed well. One of the most accomplished modern versions of what is now called the 'Mismatch' is that presented by the English TV magician, Paul Daniels. Part of the humour of this depends upon Daniels' superb patter, and pretended incompetence, especially when bits of the woman appear in impossible sequences. Since there are many variants on this sophisticated mismatch act, there are several ways of accomplishing it on stage. Some performers – notably David Copperfield, working in the USA – have used an unfortunate assistant who is strung from chains, upside-down, and bombarded with lasers, resulting in mismatches which are extremely funny. However, this simple solution explains what actually happens in the performance described above: What you see in the mismatched sections of the assistant are life-size photographs. This is why she is put into a trance – so that she will be completely still throughout the performance. The mismatch photographs are hung on special doors inside the cabinet.

There are several ways in which this illusion can be accomplished, though there are only two basic techniques which work well. The first technique involves keeping the woman in the boxes.

These are deep enough for her to bend down and be hidden completely in the bottom box. In this technique, there must always be a photograph in the bottom box – the audience can never see straight through it –so that the assistant can remain hidden. As required by the magician, the hinged photographs are pulled out by the assistant herself.

In the second technique, the lady is not in the boxes at all. Before the mismatching begins, she has already climbed out of them. She must do this immediately after it has been demonstrated that she is inside. The easiest way is for her to climb through a trap door, beneath the tier of boxes. Alternatively, she can slip between the curtains at the back (the back doors of the boxes must be left open to obscure this escape route). In this version, the hinged photographs are specially sprung, and released by the magician who presses secret buttons on the boxes when he opens the doors.

The main advantage of the second technique is that it permits the illusion a further development. When, at last, the magician has despaired of succeeding in properly uniting his various mismatches, he discovers that his assistant has disappeared altogether. This, of course, means that all the photographs have been removed, and each of the doors has been opened. At this point of despair, the mismatched woman walks on stage, in one piece, to the appreciative applause of the audience.

CHAPTER 8

TORTURE AND BLOODTHIRSTY TRICKS

One of the best-known illusions which magicians have delighted in staging for well over a hundred years involves sawing an assistant in half, or perhaps chopping her arm in two. Most of the following illusions are variations on this theme, and can be performed with reluctant victims, plenty of stage blood and accompanying screams, depending on how theatrical the act is to be. It can be effective to have no blood, however – illusions are just as entertaining and baffling for spectators without gory embellishments.

Cutting Through a Wrist

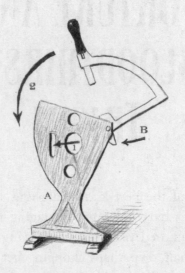

This convincing illusion need not be quite so blood-thirsty as its potential offers. However, in some performances, the limits of ordinary decency are over-stepped, and the wrist is seemingly severed, with much blood and gore. To add to the entertainment, the assistant faints – as if in extreme pain – and the magician (acting as though the trick has inadvertently gone wrong) calls out in panic, 'Is there a doctor in the house?' Here is how the trick may be performed without any unnecessary blood-letting charade.

The magician carries on stage what he calls a 'small but useful guillotine'. It is, in fact, a long, sharp knife-blade, pivoted at one end, and covered in a colourful protective casing. This has four portholes, through which it is possible to see the movement of the blade, in its sweep downwards. To show the lethal action of this diabolical machine, the magician inserts a stick of celery into the largest hole, and cuts it cleanly in half with a single sweep of the blade. This leaves the audience in no doubt about the guillotine's efficiency.

The magician's assistant is persuaded to push one of her hands into this guillotine hole. Whether or not she does so willingly depends on how dramatic the perfor-mance is to be. Once her wrist is inside, the magician takes the knife handle, and swishes the blade downwards. The audience sees the blade sweep past the portholes, yet the girl's hand remains intact. The girl removes her hand and shows it, still whole and in pristine condition, to the audience.

HOW THE TRICK IS DONE

As the magician demonstrated at the outset, the guillo-tine does have a blade capable of cutting. Fortunately for the victim, however, it is an adjustable blade, which is retractable.

The knife handle has a spring-loaded catch which allows the blade to be retracted. Before pulling down the knife, in the final chopping of the assistant's wrist, the magician pulls on the catch, so that the top half of the blade retracts into the handle. This leaves two end blades *in situ*. It is these two stumps which the audience sees moving through the portholes, and imagines to be the entire blade.

ॐ

Sawing a Woman in Half

Assistants carry on stage a substantial table. On top of this, they place a special guillotine-like contraption. The magician shows this mechanism to his assistant, and explains that he is going to try to cut her in half. He adds, almost in parenthesis, that this performance is something of an experiment, because he has never before attempted to use an electric saw on a woman. He also suggests that any member of the audience who does not like the sight of blood might care to leave the show at this point, or else hide their eyes.

In some acts, much dramatic effect is permitted at this stage. For example, when the magician explains that he intends to cut his assistant in half, and shows her the long-bladed electric saw, she might try to run off, screaming.

She can then be held back by others, and forced into the contraption, suitably terrified. In other acts, she might be put into a trance, and lowered into a substantial contraption by special winches.

When she is finally trapped inside, she is, of course, still partly visible. From one end protrude her head and shoulders; from the other end her feet. She is well and truly gripped in this prison, which traps her firmly around the waist. With much horrid grimacing, the magician begins to cut his assistant in half with his electric saw. She shows all signs of being terrified, and may even faint from the pain. Depending upon the nature of the trick (and the type of audience) the presentation may be very bloodthirsty.

When the saw blade has passed right through the woman's body, the audience assumes that the mutilation has been completed. However, the fully restored and smiling assistant then steps out of the contraption and takes her bow.

The magician Dunninger, who collected hundreds of tricks and illusions in his magical encyclopaedia, described a version of this illusion as 'One of the Most Mysterious Acts Which Can be Produced Either for Semi-Professionals or Amateur Theatricals'. However, in my opinion, this illusion is well beyond the ability of the amateur, if only because of the sophisticated equipment and stage assistance which it demands. This trick, in a thousand different forms, has been the staple diet of conjurers for many centuries. The modern version of the massive tree-saw, wielded by stalwart stagehands, is the power-saw. The great Swiss illusionist, Ravisoud, used an evil-looking commercial saw, with a 60-cm (24-in) blade, which cut through a box in a second! As you will see, however, the blade itself is merely a histrionic irrelevance. In a more sophisticated version of this trick, evolved by Houdini, the woman is not only severed, but cloned. At the end of the trick she is transformed into identical twins!

HOW THE TRICK IS DONE

For all the blood and entrails sometimes displayed in the more gory shows, the lady is not cut in two at all. There are several ways of sawing a woman in half in a convincing way, but the following method is by far the simplest, and is based on a relatively modern tradition, probably established in Victorian days. There is a huge variety of other elegant solutions – once the basic principles have been mastered, there is no end to the manipulations and displays which are possible. Some magicians perform the illusion fairly 'straight', but others invest the guillotine mechanism with mystery and eastern romance. In some acts, the victim is unwilling, and must be hypnotized before being lowered by chains into the casket. In other acts, she is the wrongly convicted slave-girl of a terrible eastern potentate, who is manhandled into the guillotine alive and screaming. In some sophisticated acts, a winching system is used to lift the heavy mechanism, replete with woman, into the vertical, before —or even while —the sawing takes place.

The secret of this particular illusion lies in the clever construction of the electric saw. The audience thinks that there is only one saw-blade, while the device really has two. One is set in the saw as it slides towards the body of the woman: at a prearranged position, however, the magician releases the screw at the top of this blade, and the latter drops into a compartment in the guillotine mechanism. The bladeless tool runs over the top of the prone woman, in the groove at the top of the porthole. When it has passed over the body, a small catch on the saw takes up a second blade (already mounted on the far side of the guillotine), which is automatically locked in place as the tool grips its top. It is this second blade (perhaps stained liberally with blood) which emerges from the far side of the woman, giving the audience the impression that it has passed through her.

In the older, and more familiar, performance of this trick, a woman is placed inside a box and then sawn in half. It differs from the more modern version described above in that there is one saw, but two women. The special box or casket has a set of holes, designed to reveal the two feet of the woman at one end, and her head (and even her two hands) at the other. The lower table, on which the box rests, has a hidden trough, deep enough to hide the body of a second woman, who lies prone underneath. A sliding panel gives the feet of this woman access to the lower end of the casket. In performances where the magician has shown the table to be empty, by thrusting his sword through the top, there are two ways of ensuring that the lady finds her way into the table trough. After the spearing of the table, she can creep through on a special board, projecting from the back curtain, while a piece of misdirecting is done onstage. Alternatively, she may be carried onstage in the casket. In this case, the casket, as well as the table, has a sliding panel to allow her to exit. Yet another arrangement is for the casket to have a series of transverse bars along its bottom. These permit the assistant to be carried in, yet leave her free to open the table panel, and slip into the table trough.

At the beginning of the performance, the first lady – the ostensible victim – climbs into the casket in full view of the audience. She pushes her head through the top hole. At the same time, the hidden woman pushes her feet through the holes at the other end. Timing must be exact, to suggest that this double action is really the action of a single woman. As soon as the lid has been put down, the victim lifts her knees over her chest, thus ensuring that her body is pushed into the top part of the casket. At the same time she pushes her hands through the pair of top holes.

Naturally, the magician can saw through the casket with alacrity, because there is a considerable space between the two women. If 'blood' is required, this is obtained by pasting a plastic sack of stage blood along the line of the saw-cut, about a third of the way down the casket, on the side facing the audience.

❧

Beheading a Woman

The magician carries onstage a simple guillotine, and demonstrates how it works to his assistant and the audience. When the handle of the mechanism is pressed down, the audience sees the passage of the blade as it sweeps through the neck-aperture, and the smaller holes alongside. He may even go so far as to chop in two a cabbage, or some other vegetable, to show how ferociously the device cuts.

The magician persuades his assistant to put her delicate neck through the guillotine hole and plays up the dramatic implications of this to the full. When her head is securely in the hole, the magician pushes down the sharp blade. The audience sees the blade sweeping past the side holes, yet the girl's neck remains unsevered, and her head stays attached to her body.

This particular version of the performance does not exploit the act's potential for blood-spilling. In the hands of a monster-magician, this could be the most bloodthirsty of all the acts in his repertoire. However, there is something more compelling in playing this illusion straight, or even dead-pan, when its capacity for blood-letting is so obvious to the audience. Refinements may be added, however. For example, the magician could mesmerize his assistant in order to get her to put her head into the hole, and so on. On the whole, most audiences prefer the entertaining to the gory.

HOW THE TRICK IS DONE

The secret of this illusion rests on the nature of the extractable cutting blade. There are really three blades – or, more precisely, one whole blade and two quarter ones. When the guillotine and its extractable blade are exhibited in the first stage of the trick, or when the device is used to cut a cabbage, then a longer blade is used. On these occasions, the blade is clipped firmly into the lower part of the cutting section. When it is in this position, it hides the obtruding two quarter blades. However, when the assistant has placed her neck in the hole, the magician flicks away the clips to release the whole blade. This drops out, and remains hidden in a slot in the top of the guillotine.

The two other 'cutting' sections are fixtures, which remain in place during the illusion. It is these which the audience sees through the side holes, next to the neck-hole. The audience, taking these blade sections for the whole blade, imagines that the descending blade is cutting through the neck of the unfortunate girl.

༄

Maiden Put to the Sword

A large upright cabinet is wheeled onstage. A separate table, with a pile of swords on it, is carried onstage, and placed alongside. The magician opens the door of the cabinet, to reveal that the door and the sides of the cabinet are perforated with slits. He explains that this casket is a modern version of the old Iron Maiden, which was used to put witches to death. As he speaks, he passes a sword through one pair of side-slits, to show that anyone standing inside would be stabbed. A member of the audience is invited to inspect the cabinet and swords.

Now the magician's assistant comes on stage, and is persuaded to enter the casket. She fits snugly inside, with very little room to spare. With devilish glee, the magician closes the door on her. He padlocks the cabinet, and perhaps locks chains around it, assuring the audience that she cannot possibly get out.

With a deliberate movement, the magician chooses a sword, and thrusts it through the casket at a point which would surely go right through the girl's heart. There is a terrible scream, and blood begins to trickle from the cabinet. The magician is without mercy. Systematically, he thrusts sword after sword through the sides, until there is silence – though no lack of blood.

EGYPTIAN HALL

DAILY AT 3 & 8

MODERN WITCHERY

THE MIRACLE OF LH'ASA

When the available swords have been used, the magician pulls them out, complete with bloodstains. When all have been removed, he opens the cabinet door, and – to the astonishment of the audience – the woman steps out, unscathed.

HOW THE TRICK IS DONE

This illusion may be performed in a number of different ways. The cabinet may be a fairly straightforward box, with the slits for the swords edged in steel, or it may be a model of the famous Iron Maiden of Nuremberg, which really was used for investigative torture well into the 18th century, and was a tourist attraction until it was destroyed by Allied bombing in 1944.

Whatever the design, it is as well to have the cabinet raised on legs. Otherwise the audience will suspect that the woman has somehow escaped, through a trap door. Also, it needs to be big enough for the girl inside to move around to some degree – indeed, the assistant's adroit movement is the essence of this illusion.

Depending upon how bloodthirsty this act is to be, the illusion can cause a sensation. In some performances, members of the audience have actually fainted, so convincing is the illusion of murder. Of course, it is quite possible to tone down the blood and screams. Whatever your preferences in blood and gore, this is how the above illusion is worked.

The secret lies not in the cabinet, as the audience believes, but in the design of the swords. Each sword used has a blade which is detachable just a little way down the shaft. When a sword is pushed into the cabinet, the assistant snaps it off before it touches her. In a secret drawer at the top of the cabinet is a set of special sword points, a few inches long. Having 'broken off' the sword blade, the assistant merely inserts the blooded point through the correct hole on the other side of the cabinet.

The key to this trick lies in the regulation of movement, so that the breaking of the sword and the following emergence of its end-point is done in a rhythmic sequence which maintains the illusion of there being only a single sword. The whole illusion is worked by split-second timing, and a thorough awareness of the order of insertions. Needless to say, the false swords are not those displayed to the audience. If the whole set of swords has been offered for display, a switch must be made with the trick set before the illusion is performed.

When the time comes for the swords to be removed, the assistant brushes them with stage blood, and locks each blade onto a hilt. As the swords are gently eased out by the magician, she pulls out the corresponding tips at the same time.

∽

The Wicker Basket

The magician and his assistants, all in voluminous robes, haul onstage a huge wicker basket. They spread a carpet on the floor, and lift the basket onto it (to show the audience that this is no mere trap-door trick).

Making much of his evil intention, an assistant drags on stage an unwilling boy. She threatens him with a curved sword, and forces the boy to climb into the basket, though he may also be persuaded to do so willingly. The assistant pushes down the lid, and either sits or stands on it, to ensure that the boy cannot get out.

Now, with bloodthirsty cries, the assistant starts to stab the sword into the basket, searching for the boy. After a couple of thrusts, there is a terrible scream from within, and the assistant pulls out the sword, which is dripping with blood. As though dissatisfied, the assistant repeats the operation. This time there is silence, but more blood. The assistant leaps from the top of the basket, and removes the lid to discover that the basket is empty. Finally, the boy, quite unharmed, enters and takes his bow.

There are many variants of this trick. Usually it is not quite so bloodthirsty, and sometimes a dog, or another animal, replaces the boy. In some stage spectaculars, the boy reappears after the seeming slaughter, floating down from the wings, to land beside the magician's assistant, and take a grinning bow. In some other spectaculars, the boy announces his presence from among the audience.

HOW THE TRICK IS DONE

The basket is just large enough to take the boy. However, it is not an ordinary basket, but has been specially prepared with a sliding bottom. To effect the illusion, all the boy has to do is drop through this hole, and leave the basket empty. The carpet has also been prepared in advance. When it is carried on, it already has a hole cut in it, but the cut-out piece has been stuck back in place with sticky tape. Although this repair job is not visible from the vantage point of the audience, it is easily pushed through. When the carpet and basket are carried onstage, they are both placed on top of a trap door. To perform the illusion, the boy simply presses his feet through the bottom of the basket and through the hole in the carpet, and drops down below stage through the trap door.

Another version of the trick involves the boy forcing his way through the wicker at the back of the basket. While the magician or the assistant is thrusting the sword in all directions – thus drawing the attention of the audience – the boy crawls through the back of the basket and hides under the robes of an assistant. After that, there is a choice: he may crawl behind other assistants to escape by way of the back curtain. Alternatively, he can remain hidden in the robes, to return eventually to the basket, and be pulled offstage, after the illusion is completed. If the latter procedure is adopted, there is a second boy, a double, who runs onstage to take the bow, or who unobtrusively becomes a part of the audience, to reveal himself when the trick is almost at an end.

Apparently, when Indian fakirs do this trick in the open, with the audience gathered around in a circle, the escape route is not so easy. Those who have studied fakir magic say that, in some cases, the rural equivalent of a trap door is used – the basket is placed over a hole, which leads to a small cave-like hideout below ground. The boy slips through the bottom of the basket, drops down the hole, and hides in this, to give the impression of having disappeared.

In another fakir version of the illusion, the boy curls round the inside edge of the basket while the fakir is stabbing through the top and sides. Split-second timing allows the boy to manipulate his position, according to the known sequence of strokes. Thus, the boy remains in the basket, but is not harmed by the seeming savagery. In any performances, onstage or in the open, if there is blood, it is stage-blood, in carefully hidden plastic sacks.

ɔ⍺ᴐ

Shooting Through the Heart of a Girl

Onstage is a large steel plate, covered with a thick piece of wood. These, as the magician explains to the audience, are designed respectively to stop and to absorb a bullet. As he speaks, he brandishes an evil-looking gun. In front of the steel plate is an ordinary shooting target. In front of this is a table with a glass of water on it. The magician directs an assistant to stand in front of the target and the glass of water. It can add to the drama if she is wearing a dress with a target decoration over her heart.

The magician takes up the gun, and with much show loads the breach. He aims the gun at the girl and carefully adjusts his position so that the centre of the target and the glass are in line with her heart. Once he is satisfied that the sight is aligned, he fires the gun.

Immediately, the blast shatters the glass, sending water everywere, but the assistant is quite unharmed, even though the bullet appears to have gone right through her. The magician retrieves the bullet from where it is lodged in the back safety screen. Meanwhile, the assistant pulls the target from its holder, and shows the charred bullet hole to the audience.

This remarkable trick may not seem to be suitable for amateurs – most tricks involving guns are best left to the professionals, for they usually demand great expertise. Although this is the realm of illusion, it is important to remember that some gun-shot tricks really do depend upon skill. One marksman, Adolph Topperwein, performed similar shooting tricks for a period of 12 days. During this time, he fired at over 72,000 rapidly moving targets, and missed only six of these. However, several highly proficient magicians have met an untimely end as a result of accidents during shooting tricks. The famous Chung Ling Soo – who was actually a New Yorker named Elsworth Robinson – was famous for his trick of catching a discharged bullet in his teeth. He performed the trick thousands of times, yet died in 1918 when a gun was fired in error. This should at least curb any amateur enthusiasm for that particular trick.

HOW THE TRICK IS DONE

In magic, things are rarely what they seem to be. This particular illusion can, in fact, be staged by amateurs with assistants, for the truth is that no bullet is shot from the gun at all – and no bullet is loaded into the gun to start with. After firing the gun, the magician palms a spent bullet, which he contrives to pick out of the wood behind the target.

There are two mechanisms upon which the trick depends. The first ensures that the glass shatters when the gun is fired. The glass is placed in a very precise position, over a hole, so that it is beneath a simple mechanism which releases a heavy steel ball from above, and which is operated by an accomplice offstage. When the ball drops, it shatters the glass, spills the water, and lodges itself in the hole beneath the glass. The resulting debris is sufficient to hide the hole from the view of the audience.

An alternative glass-breaker is a spring-loaded hammer-head, so arranged that when it is released, it strikes against the glass in the same direction as the supposed movement of the bullet. This is also operated by an accomplice, who is hidden under the table and who pulls the hammer out of sight immediately after the strike.

The target in front of the glass serves a double purpose. First, it acts as a protection for the girl, and ensures that she will not be hit by fragments of flying glass. Second, it offers visible confirmation that the bullet, which did not harm the girl, has been fired.

The hole through the target, which is offered as proof that a bullet was fired, is made by a second mechanism. Although it looks two-dimensional from the audience's viewpoint, the board on which the target is mounted is a narrow, hollow compartment. Once again a spring-loaded mechanism is involved, but this time, in place of a hammer-head, there is a sharp rod, the same diameter as the supposed bullet. Released by the accomplice beneath the table, this makes one strike through the back of the target-board (which already has a hole in it, to facilitate the movement), and continues through the front of the target. The assistant quickly withdraws the rod, so that there is no chance of the audience seeing it. All that it leaves is a hole in the target.

This puncture is clearly made from the back of the target, outwards – in the opposite direction to the path traced by the bullet. If examined closely, this would give the game away. While from a distance no one will be able tell from which direction the hole was made, a closer examination will reveal the direction quite clearly. Fortunately, however, this is no ordinary target – it is printed with the same concentrics back and front. Therefore, when the assistant removes the target, she merely turns it round before displaying it to the audience. An astute magician will also have impregnated the tip and sides of the hammer-head with carbon powder, to leave no doubt about whether a bullet was fired.

CHAPTER 9

SENSATIONAL ILLUSIONS

When magic is worked on a grand scale, or involves complicated vanishing tricks, it always seems to cause more amazement and wonder among an audience than might be expected. Surprisingly perhaps, even when an illusion is performed in a spectacular way, it is often just a variation on a trick which can be done on a small scale. The following illusions are beyond the means of an amateur, simply because of the elements involved. The thing to remember when trying to work out how similar illusions are staged is that the magic really lies in what you cannot see, rather than what you can.

❧

The Disappearing Fire-engine

This is one of the standard 'astounding spectaculars' – many professional magicians have a variation of it in their repertoire, and it is based on a relatively simple technique. The truth is that any really proficient magician can make anything vanish in such a way, but for the trick to be effective, a great deal of showmanship is required. In Victorian times, the favourite vanishee was a mounted horse. The great magician, Howard Thurston, was especially famous for his disappearance of a white car – a Whippet which was usually filled with half a dozen glamorous beauties.

Today, a fire-engine makes the stunt most impressive. Before he begins the trick, the magician takes the audience into his confidence, declaring that although inferior magicians might use trap doors to make things vanish, he would never stoop to such a level. He announces that he will now make a huge fire-engine disappear – and says again that there is no possibility of a trap door being used as an escape route.

To prove his point, a substantial trestle is brought onstage, and a member of the audience is invited to inspect it. The stagehands attach to this a special sloping board, which gives access to the platform. With much fanfair, a brightly coloured fire-engine, its lights flashing and siren blaring, is driven in and up the access board, carefully coming to a halt on the trestlework. To add to the dramatic effect, the motor is left running.

Stagehands then carry off the access board, and a coloured curtain, wider and taller than the fire-engine, is lowered, so that the fire-engine is hidden from the audience's view.

Although a curtain has dropped, the trestlework still remains visible, to reassure the audience that no trap door can possibly be used. The audience is also under the impression that they can see the space above the curtain, as before. The dropped curtain remains in place for only a second or two. The audience can hear the motor running, and perhaps also see the exhaust fumes, still emitting from the side. The magician fires a pistol, and the curtain rises to reveal that the fire-engine has disappeared. Sometimes, it adds to the excitement if the stupefied driver is left sitting in a daze on the trestle.

HOW THE TRICK IS DONE

Although this may not be exactly how Thurston made his white car disappear, it is how the New York magician, Joseph Dunninger, worked the illusion before dignitaries such as Roosevelt, Taft, Woodrow Wilson, Coolidge and even Thomas Edison. The trestlework is genuine, and the magician's patter about the stage trap door is also genuine. The fire-engine, however, disappears not into the bowels of the theatre but into the flies above the stage.

The vehicle is hoisted by a counterweighted mechanism, which is operated by a noiseless windlass. As soon as the curtain descends, six chains drop from the flies, and are attached by stagehands to six hooks underneath the vehicle. Immediately, the fire-engine is hoisted upwards, above the drop curtain. As it is lifted, its transit upwards is hidden behind black velvet. This black curtain may be raised at the same time as the fire-engine, and its movement will be quite invisible against the background of the stage backcloth behind, provided that this is very dark – preferably black. Any scenery must be very bright in hue, as must the fire-engine. The white Whippet used by Thurston was an ideal colour. This contrast is necessary to give an almost dazzling effect against the black. Front lighting and illumination from the footlights will also obscure the use of dark curtains, and the duplicitous black velvet.

When the pistol shot is heard, the fire-engine has already 'disappeared', though in reality it is still being trundled up by the mechanical winch towards the flies.

☙☞

The Vanishing Elephant

This effective illusion has been widely practised in one form or another since mid-Victorian times. It requires considerable preparation, and is obviously well beyond the capability of any amateur other than one who is friendly with a zoo-keeper, and has a large stage on which to perform!

First, this is how the illusion is performed with a real elephant. Imagine that on stage is an enormous wooden crate, with an open top. It is strongly built on all sides, but the front section has a hinged half door, or a door that may be dropped from the flies above the stage. This crate stands on a well-constructed trestle, so that the audience may see underneath it. Members of the audience are invited to walk around the crate to confirm that it is sound.

The magician explains that he will arrange for a mahout to lead his elephant into the crate. Once they are inside, stagehands will nail up the door, and shore up the front to ensure that the elephant is completely restrained. Then he will make both elephant and mahout disappear.

An elephant is led in by the mahout to a great fanfare. The mahout climbs onto the elephant's back and it walks slowly up a ramp into the crate. The elephant trumpets, and either the door is lowered from the flies above the stage, or stagehands hammer long nails into the hinged door. The elephant and mahout are now out of sight. The elephant can be heard trumpeting inside the crate, which begins to sway. Then there is a sound of battering from the inside, as though the animal is trying to smash its way out. The magician appears to be frightened, and makes a pass with his magic wand, at which point the noise and the movement subside.

Using electric saws, the stagehands quickly cut away the planks at the front of the crate (or the lowered door is raised once more). The crate is revealed to be empty and the elephant and the mahout have indeed disappeared.

HOW THE TRICK IS DONE

Like many good illusions, it is all done with mirrors – or, more precisely, with a mirror. The main source of the illusion is the trestlework. Although the audience has the impression that there is a space underneath the crate, through the trestlework, this is not the case. A mirror has been placed behind the first few trestles, at such an angle as to give the impression of further trestlework and curtains beyond. This optical illusion is created because the mirror reflects the bottom of the box, where a curtain and trestlework have been fixed before the show.

Unseen by the audience, what actually happens is that the floor of the crate is lowered, and the mahout leads out the elephant under the stage. The noise of the elephant is pre-recorded. The terrible shaking of the crate is done from inside, by assistants who enter and leave the crate by the same exit as the elephant and mahout use.

ργ

How to Drown a Woman

Onstage is a giant glass aquarium. This is about 1.8 m (6 ft) high, and about 1.5 m (5 ft) square at its base. The magician, or his assistant, drops the end of a hose over the top, and begins to fill the tank with water. While it is filling, the magician entertains the audience with a few small-time tricks. Alternatively, he might like to invite members of the audience to examine the aquarium, to ensure that there is no trickery. The illusion will certainly be more spectacular if people are seen walking around the tank, ensuring that it really is being filled with water.

When the aquarium is about half full, a ladder is brought on stage, and a female assistant enters wearing a dressing gown, which she strips off to reveal a swimming costume. At a sign from the magician, she climbs the ladder, and jumps into the tank. The water eventually settles – the level is above her waist. Meanwhile, water continues to pour from the hose into the tank.

Stagehands place a transparent cover over the top of the tank, and screw it down. It has a small vent to allow air to escape, but the woman is clearly a prisoner in the aquarium. She swims around but it is evident that soon the water will reach the top, and she will not be able to keep her head above water. She looks bound to drown, as her frightened gestures indicate. The magician pulls a curtain to obscure the tank from the audience's view. A second or so later, the curtain is drawn back – to reveal that the woman has vanished!

This daring trick is capable of much dramatic refinement and development. For example, the assistant could be provided with a pair of goggles and a breathing apparatus. During the act, the apparatus might 'break down', so that she appears to genuinely be in trouble. Naturally, the magician will fail to observe this, because he is intent on entertaining the audience, and he will feign deafness to all entreaties. The act could be carried so far that the girl may even appear to drown, as the water finally laps over the top of the aquarium.

Not surprisingly, this trick requires careful preparation, and should be avoided by any amateur keen to avoid going to jail for manslaughter!

HOW THE TRICK IS DONE

Professional magicians perform this trick using two tanks. A second tank, about the same size as the one seen by the

audience, is offstage, behind the curtain, and is filled with water at the same time as the tank onstage. The bottoms of these two tanks are connected by a rubber pipe which is wide enough for the girl to swim through. The stage aquarium is fitted with a trap door, which opens down into this pipe. When the curtain is drawn over the tank, the girl makes her escape through the trap door and swims underwater to the tank behind the curtain.

Since draining the water and dismantling the tanks takes a considerable time, it is best if this illusion is performed as a finale. Alternatively, the act should be positioned towards the back of the stage, so that a curtain may be drawn to obscure this procedure, once the illusion is over. The performance may then continue, nearer the proscenium, while the tanks are dismantled.

In some shows a dramatic feature is made of the relative immobility of the tank. For example, once the act appears to be over, and the magician is already involved in some other minor trick, an assistant may pull a screen across the tank, as though to hide it for the remainder of the performance. This screen obscures only the lower part of the tank, however, and a moment or two later, the girl reappears in the tank (perhaps with just her head visible above the screen).

This 'second' appearance may even be used as a trick distraction, or useful misdirection. Whether the girl in the tank disappears again, or is helped out of the tank, is up to the magician. An excellent dramatic effect is for the magician to pretend not to be aware of the girl this second time – she is seen only by the audience. This is an effective stratagem, since the audience is left with the conviction that she is still in the tank, even when she is no longer visible, hidden by the screen. In reality, of course, she will have escaped once again by way of the hidden connecting pipe.

If this act is to be a grand finale, the magician might choose to fill the tank not with a hose, but by magic. For instance, he might use a large version of the well-known Magic Tap. This tap is not connected to anything – there is no plumbing. The tap is screwed into the side of the tank, with the outlet on the inside, connected to nothing other than thin air. Members of the audience may examine it, and will detect no trick. When the tap is 'turned on', however, the water appears to flow from it, even though there is no supply pipe. In fact, what the audience sees as water streaming downwards is water being squirted upwards in a fine jet towards the tap outlet.

❧

Vanished by Clowns

The curtains rise to reveal four outrageously dressed clowns. Each is carrying the corner of a large sheet of plate glass. There is some grimacing and fooling from the clowns, who seem to object to their load. However, the magician walks up to each of them, and touches their heads with his wand. As he does so, the clowns freeze, with bizarre expressions on their faces.

The magician's female assistant climbs on to the glass bed, and lies down. Another assistant, helped by the front clown, then holds up a large cloth for a moment or two, so that the girl cannot be seen by the audience. After only a few seconds, and with a dramatic flourish, the cloth is pulled back to reveal – nothing! The girl has disappeared and the clowns, who unfreeze and appear to be astonished at what has happened, are left holding just the empty sheet of glass. Before shuffling offstage, the clowns may do a little act – the odd somersault, and so on, as befits their boisterous nature. As a finale, they may run back onstage, cheerfully carrying the assistant who vanished on their shoulders.

This is a version of one of Houdini's most remarkable tricks. Instead of clowns, Houdini put onstage ostentatiously robed Indian gentlemen carrying the sheet of glass. It was a performance worthy of his inventive genius. In fact, the trick is so elegant that it is unlikely that we would know how it was achieved, had Houdini not left notes explaining his original illusion.

HOW THE TRICK IS DONE

An essential part of this trick is that the clowns are not seen to walk onstage – they are 'discovered' when the curtain rises. This is necessary simply because one of the clowns cannot walk – it is a fake, hollow model. When the cloth has been raised to obscure the reclining assistant, she quickly gets off the glass and slips inside the hollow clown through an aperture in its back. Thus, the girl then becomes the animating force within the fake, so that when the disappearance has been effected, the clown can fool around, and walk off, along with the other three. In order for the girl to reappear onstage, safe and sound, there must be a 'fifth' clown, ready and waiting in the wings in exactly the same costume as the fake clown.

With a great deal of care, the act may be done using a bed, rather than the plate glass, which perhaps is more in keeping with the nature of clowns. However, this means that music and drum-rolls will probably be required to obscure any noise from the springs when the girl climbs off the bed. If music is not possible, a more substantial base may be required – a ladder is a suitable substitute.

By now, it must be obvious that the trick is done with clowns because of their capacious and baggy clothes. Large heads, masks and hats, bulbous noses, baggy trousers, and great flat feet, or thick coloured socks are all ideal disguises for the fake clown which is to be animated by the assistant. It is for the same reason that Houdini chose voluminously dressed Indians, with turbans, baggy trousers, and so on. Other imaginative alternatives, from pirates to humans dressed in animal costumes, could just as easily be used.

Naturally, the fake clown must be substantial enough, and sufficiently well-constructed, to bear part of the weight of the assistant. The quality of acting must also be taken into account: in order not to draw attention to the immobility of the fake clown, the others must keep reasonably still. This is one reason why the magician 'freezes' the clowns – to reduce the three live clowns to the same level as the fake. Too much movement from them will reveal the fake to be a very dead clown indeed. The fake clown can also be hidden, to a large extent, if one of the other clowns stands between it and the audience.

To some extent, the magician can get around the problem of the fake's immobility by arranging for it to be a simple marionette. Nothing very complex is required for the illusion to be convincing – it is sufficient for its shoulders to move slightly, and for its head to swing round, perhaps to grin at the audience. A mark of genius would be to arrange the marionette strings so that the fake can scratch its head with one hand, while the other hand supports the weight of the bed.

CHAPTER 10

THE END OF THE SHOW

As an entertainment draws to a close, it is exciting for the audience if the last act is both unexpected and memorable. The following two illusions are relatively simple to stage and can create a lasting impact on the audience. Both involve, in theory, the removal of a head. In the first illusion, the magician appears to take off his head and hand it to his assistant. In the second, the assistant's head is magically removed from the top of her body to reappear on a nearby table. Although both illusions involve meticulous advance preparation, they are not beyond the limits of an amateur magician performing onstage.

Bloodless Self-decapitation

The performance is at an end. The magician bows, and exits – still bowing and facing the audience – through the closed curtains behind him. As the clapping continues, he puts his head through the curtains once more, smiles, and signs for the curtains to be drawn again. It seems that he is preparing to give an encore.

The curtains open once more to reveal the magician smiling at the audience. Alongside is one of his assistants. As the magician smiles, he lifts his hand as though to doff his cap, or take a salute. Instead, he takes off his head. Deliberately, he hands this to his assistant. As she receives it, the curtain falls for the last time.

This is a most amusing way of bringing a performance to a satisfactory finale, and seems to have been used frequently in former times, where something special was demanded to end a series of illusions. Records of shows given in the famous House of Magic, the Egyptian Hall in Piccadilly in 1879, show a full programme of delights, including a levitation, an automatic talking parrot, a dancing walking stick – all rounded off by George Alfred Cooke, Maskelyn's assistant in magic, enfolding his own head in his arm, to take the final bow.

HOW THE TRICK IS DONE

Immediately the magician has exited, and the curtains have been drawn, a headless dummy is placed in front of an inner black curtain, where it is hidden from view of the audience until the outer curtains are drawn again. This dummy is mounted against a board with a semicircular contour, which runs from just below the magician's shoulders, in a steep curve towards the level of the assistant's hands. This board is covered in black cloth of the same type as the backing curtain, to ensure that the whole board is invisible to the audience.

The form of the headless dummy is designed to be as near as possible a replica of the magician after he takes his last bow. The live magician, standing behind the screen, and in front of the curtain, places his head on the neck of the dummy, to complete the figure. The semicircular contour is so designed as to allow the higher edge to stand slightly below the level of the dummy's neck: the magician rests his own neck on the board while presenting his head as a completion of the dummy. When the curtains are drawn, the combination of dummy body and live head has all the appearance of being a complete man – the familiar magician of the show.

The left arm of the dummy is hinged at both the elbow and the shoulder, while its hand is attached to a string, the other end of which reaches the chin of the magician. When the magician pulls the string, the arm bends, and the hand reaches for his chin, and cups it as though lending it support. Maintaining this relationship between false hand and live head, the magician lifts his head slightly, to sever it from the body, and then swings it to follow the contour-arc of the board in front of him, so that his head is directed towards the hands of his assistant.

As she takes the head, the magician can thrust it out more towards the audience, for any movement in the curtain over the protective screen will now be well hidden by the assistant's body. The false arm, pulled towards the chin by the string, follows this movement, and lends a convincing illusion of carrying the head towards the assistant. As soon as the assistant is safely holding the head, the curtain is drawn, while the power of the illusion is still electrifying the audience.

The illusion as described here requires sophisticated and expensive model-work. The arm is the real problem, because if the model is not well designed, its movement may look so awkward as to give the game away. Amateurs who are interested in performing this illusion are advised to ignore the movement of the arm altogether. It is a relatively simple matter to allow for the head to 'lift of its own accord', and slide in a gentle arc towards the outstretched arms of the assistant. This has a more ghostly feeling about it, of course, and makes for just as dramatic an ending.

Whether the act is done with a moving arm, or with a floating head, it is important that the illusion is completed quickly. Half its effect depends on an element of surprise. Even as the curtains fall together, the magician steps between them, head back in place, and takes his final bow.

Crude as this description may sound, the illusion is most compelling in the softly dimmed lights of a theatre. For all its simplicity, it is probably the most dramatic of the Black Magic illusions, equalled in sophisticated elegance only by the next trick, which is an alternative finale, designed to attract justifiable applause.

❧

Removing a Head with a Mask

In this illusion, the magician's assistant takes the final bow. On stage, alongside her, is a table on which there is a mask and a feather boa. Having taken the bow, the girl picks up the mask and feathers, and holds these in front of her face for a second or two. When she puts them back on the table, her own head has disappeared. Then she holds the mask upright in the centre of the table. When she lifts this up again, her own head is on the table in its place. The curtains are drawn to rapturous applause. This is a really stunning way of ending a performance, but although it may appear to depend upon the same device as the preceding illusion, it is worked in quite a different way.

HOW THE TRICK IS DONE

There are two girls. Dress, facial make-up and wigs, if necessary, ensure that the two are sufficiently alike to be confused, especially in dim theatrical lighting. The audience is already familiar with one of the girls, for she has been the magician's chief assistant throughout the act. They will have been programmed to accept the idea that there is only one girl, and the illusion relies heavily on this acceptance.

The second girl is the one who comes on stage to take the 'final' bow, at the start of the illusion. This is excellent theatre, since the audience's attention will be on her for only a few seconds, and everyone will assume that this is the familiar girl who has participated all along.

After only a brief moment onstage, the double lifts the mask and feathers from the table, and holds these so that the mask is towards the audience, hiding her face. This is the last that is seen of the 'twin'. In the next moment, a special black bag is dropped over her head, from above. The bag is lowered into place some time before this particular illusion begins. It cannot be seen by the audience, because it is matt black – exactly the same colour as the curtain behind it. When she removes the mask from in front of her face, the girl will appear to the audience to have lost her head. The presumption is that she is carrying this along with the mask and feathers.

The headless double places the mask back on the table, holding it upright as though it were a living head. At the very beginning of this act, the original assistant crawls through a hole in the curtains, so at this point she is already sitting underneath the special table, on which the mask was first placed. As soon as her headless double places the mask and feathers on the table, the original girl thrusts her head through a hole in the table-top, face towards the audience. Her body is entirely invisible to the audience, and her head cannot be seen until the mask is lifted.

The girl's body is hidden by the curious design of the table. Between the two front table-legs are two sheets of matt black card. The audience thinks that it can see underneath the table, but this is not the case – what they see is a sort of illusion-reversal of the table trick on page 158. Because of this, the girl can sit under the table, and remain invisible.

When the double lifts the mask to reveal the original assistant's head, the impression is that her own head (that is, the head of the twin) has been severed, and lifted behind the mask to rest on the table.

As with the preceding trick, it is a good idea for the curtains to fall rapidly, before the full shock experienced by the audience is over, and before anyone considers looking more carefully at the headless body and the bodiless head. There may be a moment of stunned silence as the curtains draw together, yet enthusiastic applause is guaranteed within a few seconds.

GLOSSARY

———◆———

The following is not a complete list of all the special terms which magicians may use – they are merely the ones with which readers may not be familiar, or which appear in this book.

BANK OF THREE

One of the specialist FORCING PACKS.

BESAUTE

See STRIPPER PACK.

BLACK ART

A term relating to tricks and illusions which rely on a contrast between the light thrown upon the objects or persons participating in the performance, and the black (usually velvet) background against which they perform. The term, which may unfortunately be confused with the Black Magic, or Nigromancy, of the occult schools, was originally 'Modern Black Magic'. These performances, staged at Maskelyne's Egyptian Hall, involved 'spiritualist manifestations'. Usually these were white-draped, gauzy visitors from the Other Side – in other words, stage ghosts, spirits and phantasms.

BODYLOAD
See LOAD.

CHAMBER LOAD
See LOAD.

FALSE BOTTOM

A term used by magicians, often in a contemptuous way, to describe tricks which work on the 'false bottom' principle. Many conjuring tricks depend on the fact that boxes used in performances have secret compartments, or false bottoms, in which objects may be hidden. Of course, objects may also be produced from these compartments, so long as they have been hidden in place before the show. 'False Bottom Magic' is the equivalent of 'amateur magic'. Even so, many high-quality tricks and illusions depend upon false bottom deceits, and simple mechanical contrivances.

FEINT

A movement made to mislead the audience and distract everyone's attention.

FLASH PAPER

A specially impregnated paper which flashes when lighted with a match.

FORCE

In a card trick, the force is the card which a member of the audience takes as a result of forcing by the magician.

FORCING

A trick with cards, whereby a person is induced to take a particular card, or set of cards, when he or she believes that they are making a free choice. Forcing may be done by SLEIGHT of hand, or by means of a special FORCING PACK.

FORCING PACK

A special deck of cards designed to ensure that a person takes a particular card, even when he or she thinks they are exercising a free choice. There are several different packs available commercially. One set consists of 51 cards of the same designation, with just one different card, which is kept on top. This is intended to mislead the casual observer into thinking that the cards in the pack are all different. Another forcing pack is the 'Bank of Three'. In this the 51 cards are divided into three groups of 17. For example, there may be 17 Queens (all of Hearts), 17 fours (all of Spades), and 17 eights (all of Diamonds). Before the member of the audience is allowed to take from the pack 'any three cards', the conjuror arranges them in groups of three, 17 times throughout the pack. Naturally, he has capped these three groups with the single outsider card, to suggest that the pack is a complete one. By this stratagem, the magician knows in advance which three cards are selected.

There is another way (more bewildering to the audience) to elicit three cards from the 'Bank of Three' pack. Each of the 17 cards are grouped together. The magician offers the fanned set to three different members of the audience, ensuring each time that the relevant arc of cards is fanned in order to force each of the three different cards. Even when three people make their 'random' selection, the identity of the cards is known to the magician.

An ideal Forcing Pack is the SVENGALI DECK, in which alternate cards are identical.

FRENCH DROP

A SLEIGHT of hand in which an object appears to have been plucked from one hand by the other, but is actually left in the first hand all the time.

GIMMICK

A concealed piece of apparatus, which is needed in the performance of a trick. See also GIZMO.

GIZMO

A piece of apparatus which appears to be necessary in the performance of a trick, but which is (usually) required to hide a gimmick, which is essential to the trick.

HOULETTE

A word derived from French applied to indicate a special apparatus for displaying cards. The term seems to have been used in magic circles for those contrivances which have special pistons in the upright support, which will operate a specially prepared deck (see RISING CARD) in order to make a chosen or predetermined card rise from the pack. Such a houlette has the same effect as when a magician forces cards to rise by using his fingers.

KEY CARD

A card which has been marked by the magician, so that he can identify it, or distinguish it from the rest of the pack.

LEVITATE

To suspend in mid-air, without any visible means of support.

LOAD

The name given to the hidden object or objects which are specially prepared for production in a trick or illusion. The load carried in a secret pocket on the person of the magician (or on an assistant) is the Body Load. The load carried in a secret container is known as the Chamber Load. The one which is carried on a SERVANTE is variously called the Servante Load, the Shelf Load, or simply, the Load.

LOAD CHAMBER

A part of a container which has been especially designed to carry some object, accessible to the magician, but invisible to the audience. The load hidden in such a way is referred to as the Chamber Load. See also LOAD.

LYCOPODIUM

A fine powder which is, in fact, the spores of the plant ('Wolfsfoot') Lycopodium. In earlier days, this was known as 'vegetable brimstone', and was used to create stage lighting. Now it is often employed as a de-wetting agent to repel water. When it is brushed on the hands, these may be placed in water and will not become wet.

MARKED

Playing cards may have been secretly marked with some identification known only to the conjurer.

MISDIRECT

To direct the attention of the audience from a particular move, SLEIGHT or object, which might otherwise reveal the secret of the trick. Sometimes, intelligent misdirection is essential to the success of an illusion.

PALMING

The art of concealing a small object in the palm, or in the fingers, of the hand, while giving the impression that the hand is empty.

PARLOUR TRICKS

A term used to denote tricks performed before small audiences, so-called because they used to be staged in the parlours of people's homes. In recent times, the term has come to be used to describe tricks of no great skill or merit.

PATTER

The magician's line of talk, during the performance of a trick. Although the word originally meant 'rapid speech' (it was derived from the way people used to recite the Lord s Prayer, the 'Pater Noster', very quickly), there is no need for stage patter to be quick-fire. A laconic, even lugubrious patter often works well. The type of patter depends entirely upon what comes naturally to the performer. There are, however, several rather obvious rules of patter which should be observed.

1 Never tell your audience what you are about to do. They would prefer to see what you do, rather than hear about it.
2 Never tell the audience what they can see. They know very well what they can see, and your words will probably make them suspicious. If you tell them that they can see an empty box, they are likely to suspect that it is really full to overflowing.
3 Try to keep your patter brief and be amusing.
4 Sound as if you believe in what you say, even though you know that the whole thing is a tissue of lies. If you do not carry conviction, your tricks will not convince.

PENCIL READING

The acquired skill of reading what a person is writing from the movement of the pencil at the moment of writing. Although a difficult art to master in connection with fluid personal handwriting, it is relatively easy to learn to pencil-read numbers as they are written down. This is because each of the ten numbers has a distinctive 'aerial pattern' in the end flourish of the pencil. Practise makes perfect – so the best way to learn this art is to persuade a friend to write numbers down, while you watch and try to 'read' the movement of the pencil.

RISING CARDS

A name given to a specially prepared deck of cards in which at least 50 have had identical rectangles cut from them. The remaining two are intended to disguise the mutilations, by being placed at the top and bottom of the pack. To the casual observer, the pack will appear to be untampered with. The purpose is almost always to make a particular card (usually a FORCE card) appear as though by magic from what seems to be a normal pack. Some rising cards have the rectangle cut from the bottom, while others have the rectangles removed from their centres. Generally, magicians use their fingers to operate the rising card, but it is possible to use a HOULETTE.

SERVANTE

A hidden shelf, on the side of a table invisible to the audience.

SLEIGHT

A manipulation, made in secret, or otherwise hidden from the sight of the audience.

SMOKE

Stage smoke is usually manufactured on a small scale, to lend verisimilitude to such things as a gun-shot. Such effects may be achieved by burning smoke tablets, which can be bought from most magic shops or stage suppliers. Special smoke machines are available for large-scale effects. When circulated by a fan, billows of smoke can also be a useful way of suggesting flames.

STRIPPER PACK

A specially cut pack of cards, all of which have been shaved at one end, giving the cards a subtle tapered effect. This tapering permits a conjurer to reverse a single card into the pack and then afterwards determine its position from feel alone. Sometimes, the Stripper Pack is called the Beseaute Pack.

SVENGALI DECK

A pack of cards in which about half are slightly shorter than the rest. Twenty-four shorter cards are identical in suite and number. Twenty-six are ordinary cards. When these are interleaved, so as to alternate in sequence, it is possible to rifle through the deck so that it appears to consist only of mixed cards. With the aid of such a pack, it is possible to perform a great number of tricks, with only very little expertise. It is an ideal FORCING PACK, since the magician can ensure that the spectator either cuts to a chosen card, or chooses a specific card. Svengali packs may be purchased in most magic shops, and usually come with details of how to use them.